Praise for David Mixner

"When I met him when he was young I thought I have never met a person whose heart burned with fire for social justice so strongly. He has never forgotten the roots of his childhood...how fortunate we are in this country at this time with all the things we have to do to have his energy, his heart, his devotion and his passion."

—President Bill Clinton

"David Mixner has won a place on the annals of a movement to free a whole segment of our people from oppression. He has touched history, and in the process contributed to changing the lives of millions. The nation has learned a lot in these years about Gay and Lesbian rights—and in a very real sense, the greatest of all our teachers has been David Mixner."

—Senator Edward M. Kennedy

"Your work has made an incredible difference to so many lives and inspired people not only in America but across the world."

—Prime Minister Gordon Brown

Praise for *Stranger Among Friends*

"Impassioned...poignantly told...[a] bittersweet political odyssey."

—Frank Rich, New York Times

"Movingly personal...intriguing and timely...only sometimes does a notable life yield a worthy memoir, and this is such an instance...*Stranger Among Friends* is an optimist's book, the achievement of a doer."

—Los Angeles Times

"An intelligent and challenging biography of contemporary America…an epic that is partly David Mixner and partly his times, and future historians will be hard pressed to understand us without reading him."

—*New York Times Book Review*

Praise for *Brave Journeys*

"Provide[s] compelling narratives of courage and tenacity, of ample inspiration and commemoration."

—*Publishers Weekly*

"Inspiring…The stories remind us of the difficulties involved in coming out publicly and the need for any community to have powerful individual examples."

—*Out Magazine*

At Home with Myself

Also by David Mixner

Stranger Among Friends

*Brave Journeys: Profiles in Gay and Lesbian Courage
(with Dennis Bailey)*

At Home with Myself

Stories from the Hills of Turkey Hollow

DAVID MIXNER

MAGNUS
BOOKS

Magnus Books
Cathedral Station
PO Box 1849
New York, NY 10025

Printed in the United States of America on acid-free paper.

First Edition

Edited by: Donald Weise
Cover by: Linda Kosarin, The Art Department
Photographs courtesy of Steven Guy

ISBN: 978-1-936833-10-813.2

To Steven Guy
Can't imagine my life without him.

Preface

Early on in my connecting to the AIDS pandemic, it became more than obvious that the cruelly insensitive response of the President and much of the government, as well as the nation, was motivated by a vicious homophobia. That, in turn, made it clear that my commitment to fighting AIDS clearly was part and parcel of my passionate involvement with the gay community in fighting for equal rights.

Almost immediately I encountered the man who would become not only my friend but an enduring source of inspiration. Knowing David Mixner is to be on the inside of history. With the utmost humility he has always talked casually about his day-to-day experiences without making an issue of the fact that he is interacting with world leaders—Presidents and Prime Ministers, influencing decisions that will impact not only the country but the world, and advising some of the most powerful political figures of our day.

There is a reason that *Newsweek* called him "the most powerful gay man in America." The history of the Democratic Party over the last several decades would be extremely different without the role played by David Mixner. He was, in 1976, one of the founders of the first gay and lesbian PACs, the Municipal Elections Committee of Los Angeles. He is widely recognized as the source of the stunning defeat of the hateful California Proposition 6, the Briggs Amendment. His introduction of Bill Clinton to the LGBT community clearly played a pivotal role in the electoral victories of 1992. It is only someone like David, however, who, despite his enduring friendship and connection with the President, refused to continue to work in the White House and chained himself to the White House fence to protest the passage of "Don't Ask, Don't Tell." Were I to focus on all of David's contributions to the gay community, I would threaten to take pages away from this wonderful book.

No discussion of the age of AIDS would ever be complete without featuring David's courageous leadership, his tireless support of literally the entire community, to say nothing of the limitless love he showed to endless numbers of those suffering from the disease—as well as their friends, lovers, and families. I doubt there is anyone who has spoken at more memorial services for people who died of AIDS than David.

He has not, however, only been involved in issues affecting the gay community. From his childhood in Southern New Jersey when he sent some of his hard earned money to Martin Luther King, Jr., there has not been an issue of equal rights that

David has not played a key role in relation to. He was one of the organizers of the Moratorium to End the War in Vietnam. His passionate support of Eugene McCarthy's presidential campaign culminated with his being one of those beaten and jailed at the 1968 Democratic Convention. Issues of poverty and hunger, and struggles against every "ism" that people are conscious enough to fight, will always find David right in the center.

The most striking thing about knowing David, however, is that the experience of this towering giant of political genius and power is quite simply one of the most humble and sweetest human beings I have ever known. "Close up and personal" he has a wicked wit and an often perverse sense of humor that keeps everyone around him in stitches.

Thankfully, this wonderful book allows David to share all of his seemingly infinite facets with a wider audience. His astonishing stories of being "behind the scenes" of history are there. So, too, is that soft-hearted animal lover who buys bushels of apples to feed his deer, allows his home and his bed to be taken over by his beloved cats, and who travels to Africa whenever he can to see the wild animals he so deeply loves in their natural environment.

If you know David, this book will remind you of all the reasons you love him. If this is your introduction to him, welcome to an experience that will open your heart and expand your consciousness.

—*Judith Light*

Introduction

Overlooking the United Nations, with the East River flowing behind it, the view from my 2,000 square foot apartment should have made me feel validated and content. After all, this was the culmination of fifty years as one of the country's best-known national political organizers. During those decades I'd worked hard to create a more just society. I'd befriended those making history and became almost family to a wide range of decision makers around the world. I'd been honored for my work and felt I'd reached a pinnacle of my career. In fact, my apartment, though only a rental, was a testament to my long career. Its spacious rooms were filled with awards, accolades, framed photographs signed by celebrity friends and other personal mementos from my extraordinary journey. Somewhere inside me these prized possessions spoke to childhood dreams of success. For a kid raised on a farm in New Jersey, this was the big league. Yet for all the pride I took in my home, possessions, and the many accomplishments they represented for me, happiness was not to be found within those walls.

When I turned sixty, a new awareness of time came over me. I began to ask myself questions about the road ahead and whether I wanted to continue along the same path. It wasn't that I didn't enjoy myself. On the contrary, my days and nights were full of laughter and good times with young people. However, there was no circle of older gay men where we would gather in each other's homes over a delicious meal, recalling hilarious stories about what fools we'd made of ourselves some summer. It was left to me to regale young gay men and lesbians with tales of our silly exploits until they begged me not to tell that oft told story one more time. These were special times of sharing fond memories with a few cherished friends, as well as a host of new ones, in warm, spirited surroundings. Still, something felt missing. It was as if I experienced these rich enjoyments only half-heartedly. Yes, something was missing—or more to the point, someone, if not some people, was missing. In fact, a lot of people were gone.

I had not expected my sixties to be a time when I would come to terms with the impact of HIV/AIDS in my life. While I knew I'd never completely reconciled the enormous pain I'd suffered from more than 300 deaths, I thought that after twenty years I had at least come to terms with it. But then the epidemic almost mandated some form of denial, if only to keep moving forward through those dark times. Otherwise how many funerals of gay men under forty years old could one person attend before losing his mind? Over time I'd attempted to make peace with the sudden loss of so many friends and loved ones—to the extent that peace under such horrific circumstances is really possible. But looking around my big apartment all those years later, I found my home empty of peers. These were supposed to be my "sunset years," the time when aged friends gather in summer rentals or travel abroad together. However, for most gay men and women my age, this was not the reality. True, many younger friends filled my life with love and friendship, but I had no real history with them. So my stories became not the familiar recollections I would have shared with peers but generational stories that a father would tell a son.

Of course, I was relieved to live into old age when so many others hadn't. How could I complain about getting old when I still had the gift of life and so many young friends to share it with? To me, any hint of self-pity was to dishonor the life I had been given, as well as the countless lives taken in the night. To not forge ahead joyfully would have been ungrateful in the most profound way, so I lived life to its fullest. I threw myself full force into presidential politics and social justice causes, I was invited to many glamorous parties, I befriended celebrities, I traveled the world, I met and fell in love with men. I couldn't have been happier, and I thought life would go on like this forever.

Around 2007 all this changed. While still socially active— more so even than many of my young friends—the desire to dance the night away or to spend weekends carousing on Fire Island was over. Truthfully, those activities had never been a driving force for me, although I enjoyed the storytelling among friends for weeks afterwards. But this transformation was as much physical as it was emotional. At sixty, the mind was sharp but the body complained. The legs were willing to make all the right moves but the muscles gave out too early. The all-nighters weren't an option anymore, so I was forced to leave this world behind—and in so doing, this world left me behind.

But with my social life now curtailed and few of my gay peers alive to keep me company, what remained, then, for someone my age?

I took stock of my situation and saw that change was in order. No longer able to rely on fun and games to engage me or to turn to my young friends for entertainment, I began to look inward. I wasn't interested in "acting my age," but I understood that the next phase of my life would need to be dramatically different from any I'd lived before if I was going to find peace of mind.

As a spiritual person, nature for me has always been a healing place. Going back all the way to my childhood on the farm, the fields and forests were places of adventure and self-discovery. Animals were companions and friends, and the world moved at a slower, more rational pace than the bustling cities where I'd resided my adult life. Yet so much of my identity was wrapped up in those cities; who and what I had become was made possible by my work in those places. Was it time at age sixty to walk away from all that? Was that option even possible? Could I return to nature, as so many others had done and written about? Embracing the idea of a Henry David Thoreau lifestyle—mixed with a little Dr. Doolittle for good measure—I made one of the boldest decisions of my life.

Turkey Hollow is a small country town in Sullivan County, a remote region of the Catskill Mountains. Surrounded by forests, it counts ten full-time residents, has no mail service and no cell phone reception. However, what it lacks in amenities, it compensates for in sheer natural wonder. The woods-scented air was fresh, there was a remarkable silence both day and night, and the night sky so clear that I felt I could reach out and touch the stars. I fell in love with the place instantly. Far from the distractions and demands of the city, I had found my Walden Pond

At the same time, by moving to Turkey Hollow I wouldn't be exactly leaving the world behind. Only two-and-a-half hours northwest of New York City, Sullivan County was full of second homes of city folks whose presence would help alleviate any sense of complete isolation. Although most part-time residents avoided the harsh winter months—which happen to be my favorite season—they return off-and-on the rest of the year for visits. Also, my friends in Manhattan who were willing to make the trek up into the mountains could see me anytime.

But before I settled in, I first needed a place to live. I found a house that was being built on a mountaintop between two peaks. It was a simple two-bedroom structure that was wired with all the modern conveniences; in short, it had my name written all over it, and I snapped it up. Once the house was completed, I painted it a cheerful bright yellow, installed a big screened porch with a fireplace out back, and completely remodeled the basement and garage to my liking. I'd come to the country to do my Thoreau bit, so I needed an office that looked out onto the woods for inspiration. I converted one of the bedrooms into my workspace and through its windows watched the wildlife appear each morning with the sunrise. Many were the day I would sit in wonder, coffee in hand, for hours.

If fellow human beings were sometimes scarce, there were always herds of deer for companions, especially an eight-point buck I fondly named Attila. Sharing the refuge of my backyard was also a couple of bears, Benny and Betty, a Bald Eagle I called Franklin, and dozens of wild turkeys—after all, this was Turkey Hollow. Hawks circled the skies and would swoop down to grab the mice that my three lazy cats had failed to notice indoors. The occasional fox, porcupine and raccoon would also pay their respects. Evenings brought spectacular sunsets along with large owls, lightening bugs and millions of stars. Often the quiet of darkness would be pierced with the cries of coyotes.

For three years this was my home. Gone overnight was the frenzied calendar of engagements, business meetings, lunch dates and deadlines. In one swift stroke I'd put an end to that way of life and not once did I regret that decision. After a lifetime I was at home with myself.

Almost from the time I settled in Turkey Hollow, I kept a journal online. If I was going to act like Thoreau, I had better write about it. Partly this was done for the benefit of city friends who thought I was nuts for packing up and disappearing into the hills. So through my entries they would be reassured to see that, in spite of talking to the animals, I had in fact held onto my sanity. But mostly the project was undertaken for myself; I not only wanted to keep a record of my new life in the country, because I felt it would be valuable to me personally, but welcomed the opportunity for reflection that writing offered. I've always loved to write and what more ideal place could there be than from a place of perfect solitude?

At Home with Myself is the story of my "wilderness years," as Gandhi referred to the moments when he retreated from the pressures of the world to contemplate matters. Unlike my autobiography, *Stranger Among Friends*, this is not a full-fledged memoir nor is this a follow up to that book. Rather *At Home with Myself* is an impressionistic record of daily life in the country as experienced by a sixty-something gay man with a love of nature, a special fondness for friends and family, a lifelong commitment to social justice and an avid curiosity.

Certainly this work shares with the autobiography my obsessions with American history and politics. However, I've refrained here from commenting on contemporary affairs, including the dynamic presidential campaign of President Barrack Obama and that of his challengers, Hilary Clinton and John McCain. Reading my comments about them today leaves me doubtful that my musings on the election are particularly valuable now that the outcomes have been decided. The same is true for electoral politics in general; in spite of the passage of controversial ballot measures like Proposition 8 in California, changes in regimes on the international front, natural disasters and at times tremendous unrest in the world, I've chosen not to speak to time-sensitive issues that have since become or in short time will become "old news."

In terms of the book's organization, *At Home with Myself* is divided into four sections, or seasons, beginning with spring. I felt it best that readers experience Turkey Hollow the way that I first did; by watching nature evolve from one magnificent seasonal landscape to the next. Although I lived there for three years and the book contains material written over that entire period, I've presented the material here as if it took place over a single twelve-month period. Otherwise the writing was burdened by repetitions, the seasons passed too quickly and the material contained lots of small details likely of interest to no one but me. However, the book, chronologically speaking, is accurate from start to finish. In spite of this small editorial reorganization, I trust the reader will enjoy the wonders and beauty of Turkey Hollow just as I did.

New York City
March 2011

Spring

On The Edge

When I was much younger, I met a poet who was in his sixties and married. He became one of my mentors in every sense of the word and to this day holds a special place in my heart. He was one part philosopher, one part poet and one part revolutionary. He breathed the fire of life. He lived life on the very edge. He pushed people publicly and privately to expand their limits and discover new dimensions of themselves.

The poet loved eccentric characters and celebrated those who saw the world in different colors. He distained consensus and believed its only purpose was to pull us down to the lowest common denominator of human thought so as not to challenge anyone. He believed deeply that if we were comfortable, we were not living. And he felt strongly that there should always be an edge to our contentment so that we wanted more out of life.

At that time in my life I had a horrible fear of heights, and I would grow shaky in the knees climbing even a stepladder.

This poet's summer home was on the Pacific Coast. We used to rock together on his back terrace, which overlooked the ocean. The lawn of sea grass stretched out about fifty yards from the terrace to a steep cliff. It was the kind of dramatic cliff you might see in a movie from which a car tumbles down and then explodes. I had no intention of ever going to the edge of that cliff. It scared the hell out of me.

The poet at that time was experiencing cancer. While he had lost much strength, he was not submissive.

One day, we were rocking on his porch, and I was tending to his needs since it was not one of his good days. We rocked quietly, looking out over the ocean at one of the most magnificent sunsets that we both had ever seen. Being with him in such beauty and quiet was a moment I will never forget.

Suddenly, he took my hand and asked me to help him out of his chair. I thought he was tired and wanted to be taken inside to rest. I helped him up and started to lead him to the door. Without a word, he turned instead to the steps leading down to the terrace toward the sea. I knew instantly what he was up to. He was going to force me to confront my fear of heights. He knew that I had a young man's ego and pride and that I was more afraid of showing fear to an elder than the origin of the fear itself. I did not want to be a coward.

Slowly and without speaking, he led me to the edge. I almost lost it and had some trouble walking. But my determination to be strong in front of him drove me on, as did his old weathered hand, which firmly held mine. It was just another lesson. The poet insisted that we not stop until our toes were on the very edge of the cliff. I could feel little stones and rocks tumble down the side, and I was sure that I would soon join them.

Finally, he spoke. "David, this is where you belong—on the edge of life. You got here by walking through your fear. You are so close to the edge that by the law of physics no one can physically stand in front of you. As a result, you have the best view of the sunset and can see colors that no one standing behind you can see."

He was silent for a long while and then continued, "This is the choice you have in life. You can walk through fear and see the colors of the sunset and describe them to others or you can hold back and have others describe the colors of the sunset to you. That is the choice."

He squeezed my hand, looked over at me and smiled and said, "It is about you experiencing life or having others tell you about life."

We walked back into the house, and I suddenly felt that the world looked different. He had given me a great gift.

Over the years, I have attempted to live my life on the edge. But living on the edge of life can be very lonely because, at times, it feels as though you are the only one willing to take a chance. I've even fallen off that damn cliff a few times.

However, it has never been boring. I'm so grateful to the old poet.

Signs of Spring

As a child waking up in the morning, the fresh smell of newly plowed fields would enter my bedroom, and at that moment I knew spring had arrived. This morning waking up in Turkey Hollow I heard the first hammering of that ever-noisy woodpecker creating new condos for all his buddies. My woodpecker community seems to tend more toward condos than individual country living. Walking in the woods, you can see a particular tree that is like the Manhattan of woodpeckers. Every once in a while you find one that prefers the splendid isolation of the forest, but that bird is clearly a hermit and has very poor social skills. And because of that, he is always the special one to me since I can identify living up in the remoteness of Turkey Hollow.

Signs of spring are everywhere.

For the first time yesterday, I could open all the windows in my house and allow the staleness of winter to escape into the crisp clean spring air. The cats, Sheeba and Uganda, inhaling deeply the bracingly fresh breeze, went crazy and started running from one end of the house to the other. You would have thought the air was filled with catnip. On the other hand, maybe it was and just undetected by us humans. They sure acted stoned out of their little kitty heads. Newcomer Kansas seems to take particular joy in reminding the older cats of the tricks of youth, and my job appears to be walking around and picking things up off the floor—a new form of spring cleaning called "picking up after the cats."

Last night the beautiful still, blue sky with blotches of red in the few clouds caught me by surprise since it was almost 8:10 P.M. before it got dark. Couldn't figure out why I hadn't noticed sooner that light was giving over to night. Soon I will be eating my meals on the screen porch, reading my favorite books and watching the deer frolic in the wildflowers. I wonder if it is time for me to get a Kindle to read by the outdoor fireplace?

The creek out back is full from the spring run-off and soon I will hear the croaking of the frogs that have deemed it safe to return after a particularly brutal winter in the Hollow. Lightening bugs can't be too far behind. Unfortunately, it also means that the hundreds of Mayflies are not too far away either. Ughh.

Our deer Kate and Attila are back and it appears that Kate is pregnant once again. What am I going to do with her? Last year we had a real chat about birth control, and when I admonished her again this year she just gave me that grin that says, "But I had one helluva of a good time with that buck…" So in just a couple of months, I will have to come up with a new name for her newborn.

With all these signs of spring, it means also taking stock of the damage of this horrible winter. A couple of doors need fixing, a panel or two on the sidewalks need repair from all the salt, porch furniture needs a steam wash, the cushions cleaned and put on the outdoor furniture and mud scraped out of the garage. Some new wildflower seeds need to be strategically placed where the snow runoff wiped out spots on the land.

However, right now all those chores can wait. With open windows, I feel the cabin fever of winter disappearing and am enjoying every sign of the freshness of spring.

Growing Up Country

Turkey Hollow doesn't present our young people with a whole lot of options for the weekend. The nearest movie is about a forty-minute drive, and the nearest town, Livingston Manor, closes up at eight sharp each night. You can drive through downtown on a Saturday night and think you have come upon a scene from the nuclear holocaust movie *On the Beach*. All that's missing are tumbleweeds blowing through the center of town.

For me, it is just fine, although I do miss the theaters. So I snuggle up with a good book, have friends in from the city for a weekend or watch the latest on DVD. But being young in such a rural and isolated environment in today's world must be tough. You often can find the local students "hanging" out somewhere. With access to the entire world via television and the Internet, it must be hard to have it so close yet so far away.

For my family, growing up country offered a lot of options—most of which would no doubt be greeted with hoots and hollers today. The early years of my life we had no television, and even when we got our first one, an amazing Philco console, it often didn't work and money to fix it didn't come easy. But it didn't matter because there was always something to do on weekend nights. In our tiny, old elementary school in Daretown, New Jersey, I remember square dances being held in our small wood-floor auditorium. Young and old alike would line up to do the Virginia Reel. Oh, how I loved to dance those evenings away as a youngster—even when I felt relentlessly silly twirling a big, overly perfumed adult woman. Indeed, for a while, being a square dance "caller" seemed like the best job in the world.

Other evenings would be covered-dish suppers at the church or grange hall—tables piled high with food from all the best cooks in the county. During the meals, laughter and lively conversation would fill the hall, followed by some form of local entertainment. Once in awhile when I was really young (back when the earth's crust was cooling) there would be a local "minstrel show" benefiting some neighborhood group. The men would appear in actual black face and full drag singing songs and attempting vaudeville-like skits. All of us would laugh until our sides ached, oblivious as to how racist these shows were. In retrospect, of course, one can look back and see how steeped in racism a community could be—behavior that seemed so innocuous and ordinary to this naive but well-meaning populace.

When Elmer Grange #29 built its big, new hall—a long white concrete block building—it became the center of community fun. Often we would have polka challenges when the ethnic city bands toured the rural areas. My sister, Patsy, and I became great polka dancers and often would clear the floor. To this day, it's still not clear if the floor was swept clean because we were so good or because we knocked all the other dancers off the floor. *Dancing with the Stars* had nothing on us, believe me. The hall would also be the place of annual benefit turkey dinners. The women would cook all week and everyone would go door to door selling tickets for a reserved place setting at the communal dinner. People, by the hundreds, would come from all over to get their all-you-can-eat turkey-with-the-fixings spread. The kids served as bus boys and waiters and everyone, at least in my happily selective memory, had a grand time.

My moment of personal glory at the Elmer Grange came when I was asked to escort and lead the dancing with Miss New Jersey Grange. It was a high local honor to be chosen to escort her majesty. My mother was so proud that I was picked to escort the beautiful visiting debutante as she made her appearance at the local hall. Mom spent the entire week explaining to me the proper etiquette toward royalty; the manners, the deference, the gallantry. Confident and beaming from ear to ear, I guided her flawlessly from the main entrance to the stage and then into the first dance. My shoes never were shined so bright, my trousers were never pleated so crisply.

My favorite nights were the Future Farmers of America's "Fun Night." On these occasions, the entire town would crowd into the small gymnasium for an evening of bucolic challenges. The greased pig contest would have us howling. As the poor, squealing pig ran around the gym, guys would attempt to catch and hold it for thirty seconds—a triumph that would accord them a bonafide win. Nowadays, I would feel horribly sorry for the pig and probably be tempted to call PETA. The greased pole contest was equally as funny and even somewhat erotic for a gay man. Guys in teams would try to climb a greased telephone pole to get the prize at the top. Shirts off, covered in grease and sweat, they would pile on top of each other in an attempt to get to the top. The cheering and laughter from the crowd raised the roof. And it was sexy to boot.

Finally, there was the big event of the summer: the Cumberland County Fair. It dwarfed all the rest of the local festivities, bar none. Tent after tent was filled with all the best baked goods, prized livestock and homemade quilts. Various games of chance and skill offered up plush, stuffed animals. But the culmination— and most envied accolade—was the Miss Cumberland County Fair contest. One especially memorable year, my sister Patsy was a contestant as Miss Seabrook Farms. My entire family, collectively holding our individual breaths, sat in the decorated grandstand, craning our necks, assessing the competition. After all, whoever won would be crowned by New Jersey's own Governor Robert Meyner. The thought of the Governor crowning our sister sent my brother Melvin and me into spasms of giggles. Unfortunately, my sister only made it to the court and just missed being Miss Cumberland County Fair. The injustice of it all. Solace could only be provided by more cotton candy and salted pretzels.

Admittedly, these recollections may have gotten a little burnished over time—smoothing over the rough patches enough to leave behind only fond memories of growing up country. Still, even in this age of iPods and iPhones, my hope is that the local youth here in Turkey Hollow are able to slow down enough to have similar experiences. My formative years as a country boy taught me a real sense of community and neighbors. It's what makes me who I was, who I wanted to be and who I am. And gave me moments to cherish for the rest of my life.

The Porcupine and Individuality

Taking a walk through my woods the other day, I noticed a huge strange presence on the path. Being in the middle of nowhere, I was extra cautious. As I approached very carefully, I realized that it was a rather large porcupine—the first one I have ever seen in the wild. It was a magnificent creature and not at all scary. With a slightly gray coat, its quills were swept backwards like the hair of a 1940s male movie star. The porcupine's aerodynamic shape would make you guess that it could get a real head of steam going, but actually it crept along at a very slow pace.

I assumed porcupines must be an endangered species since I have never seen one except in a zoo. I've come to find out that they are actually plentiful, especially in Canada. When I got home I Googled my new friend. The information on most Websites was generally the same, with very little detail. The most revealing information was that they don't actually shoot their quills but insert them into anyone who gets too close. Clearly these large rodents are loners that don't like people poking into their business. No, they move through life slowly and on their own terms.

They reminded me a lot of the mythological concept of pioneers or mountain folks who tend to be loners and ultra individualistic. After being out here in my own version of Walden Pond, I am beginning to get a sense of how that individualism and personal liberation develops in a person living fully in nature.

Nature does have its hierarchies, and each species seems to know the rules for their tribe. I have to admit that when Kate leads the deer into the woods from my backyard, I yearn for one of the little yearlings to act out and refuse to enter the woods in single file. Just once, I want to see one of them run ahead and refuse to abide by the rules.

Out here you can find yourself. You have the space, the land, the sky and the quiet to finally define yourself. And being isolated, you have the right to cling to your uniqueness without having it challenged often by others. Having that freedom, that beauty of breaking out of the cocoon of conformity is so exciting, but increasingly you feel that you just don't fit in with others as easily anymore.

Often I have said to myself that I lived the first half of my life pleasing others and the second half discovering myself. I have learned that in order to change the world and embrace our unique spiritual being, we have to liberate ourselves from the expectations placed upon us from the very early stages of life by well meaning family and friends. We have to start living our personal lives the way we want to see the world. Then we will have the first hand knowledge and experience to describe that world to others with authenticity.

In the past, I have found that I have put my life journey up to a vote of my peers in order to feel accepted by others and seek a safe place of common goals and dreams. Let's face it: society wants us all to seek the lowest common denominator of life so that we don't challenge others or make them uncomfortable. We have placed so much emphasis on acceptance by others and "comfort" that we sometimes lose our individuality.

Even in the great movements of our time that I have participated in, I've found great pressure to conform to a particular ideology and process. Just because a mass movement might represent a minority viewpoint or it is not in favor with the rest of society does not mean we have gained our own individuality. Most likely, we are just conforming within a smaller group. We still urgently want to be accepted within those movements and adopt the lifestyles or ideas of just a new, smaller tribe.

Over the last few months, I have realized that civil rights and civil liberties do not necessarily constitute complete freedom. I feel that real freedom comes from discovering our own gifts, even if they are not popular in any tribe. Freedom comes from celebrating our own uniqueness and being allowed to be eccentric and contrary. From seizing the opportunity to surrendering once again to our youthful dreams and visions of ourselves in order to finally live lives on our own terms.

I have seen all types up here including old 1960s radical fairies wanting to (still) dance naked in the woods, the quiet, long bearded, gun toting classic mountain man, the solitary poet living near a flowing brook and those who seem to be just lost in their own world of fantasy. I have met people who embrace, in some form, all of those images. But most of all, I am discovering the joy of my youthful dreams again, and I just might yet be that young deer dancing ahead to the front of the line and breaking rules.

Music and Time

Never quite figured out why, but when we had our record players in our youth they always seemed to be on the floor and in a corner. Maybe my parents felt that it would dim the ruckus that was emitting from the machines. Only our first record player was off the floor, and it played my parents' 78 records. Yes, you got that right, 78s.

As a small boy I would look through their music collection and see records from Gene Autry, The Andrew Sisters and Glenn Miller. However, with what became the first of my many young crushes on handsome young singers, Johnnie Ray's "Little White Cloud That Cried" was a song I played over and over again. Although I'm not sure what these crushes meant back then, they were strong. No muscle magazines for me, it was all about male singers. Increasingly, it was the bad boys that appealed to me the most, like Elvis Presley, Jerry Lee Lewis and Buddy Holly. Briefly, I owned a pair of white buck shoes to honor Pat Boone but quickly became bored with him. I watched *The Adventures of Ozzie and Harriet* every week just to see Ricky Nelson sing at the end of the show.

Now, the real crisis in my home came when Elvis Presley made his famous appearance on the Sunday night Ed Sullivan show. My parents were very concerned that I was not old enough to watch this "bad boy" swirl his hips. Little did they know that is exactly what I wanted to see. However, they relented when Sullivan promised to keep the camera above The King's waist and protect the sanctity of Sunday night for all American families.

As 45 records with the huge holes in the middle were at their height, once again the record player was on the floor in the corner. My sister had a huge collection of 45s but off she went to nursing school, and it was time to build my own collection. We used to jitterbug to all the hit songs until Chubby Checkers' "The Twist' came along, and I don't think dancing couples ever touched again. I loved dancing at the high school canteens, feeling totally out of control and erotic.

As I was practicing shaking my own hips, the 33 long-playing albums came out. My first ones were the folk music coming out from the "beatniks" in Greenwich Village. I loved Peter, Paul and Mary, Joan Baez, Bob Dylan and especially Phil Ochs. Their music was about justice, stopping war and resisting immoral governmental acts. But Ochs touched my heart. There was something especially soulful, haunting and wonderful about him singing about resistance to the draft with "I Ain't Marching Anymore." It turned out he later killed himself.

In the 1960s, we sang and sang during protests. In music we found strength and power and that brought us together. We were the "We Shall Overcome" generation. Often I have said that the great tragedy of the LGBT struggle for civil rights has been that we don't sing together and in the process, come together.

When the Beatles went "Sgt. Pepper" on me, it was onto the hippie era and from that onto the disco era. I did my best to keep up as I got older and tended to dress to fit the music I was listening too. But I managed to avoid long hair and white disco suits. With country music, I found my sexuality. I simply loved listening to the long, sad ballads and the songs about boozing and whoring around. From that musical style I found my fashion sense; Levi's, work shirts, cowboy boots, jean jackets, cowboy hats and even a harmonica in my back pocket. Who could be sexier than George Strait or Clint Black? After 9/11, no one captured the mood better than alan Jackson with his "Where Were You?"

One of my great fears is not being current on music. There's no question that I've fallen behind. The entire rap and punk segments of musical history have totally missed me. More and more, as I get older, I tend to listen to songs that bring back memories and put a smile on my face. However, when I watched Adam Lambert perform "The Tracks of My Tears" on *American Idol*, I was totally blown away. With his retro look and amazing vocal range, I felt not only young again but a little like a dirty old man.

God and Me

It's hard to imagine on a daily basis that there is no God. With magnificent sunrises and sunsets, the cycle of wildlife, violent storms and just plain peace in Turkey Hollow, it all seems to be part of some grand plan. Yet over the years, I have struggled to come to terms with aligning the concept of a God, my spirituality and being at one with nature. Just when I think I have some of the answers, new knowledge appears to challenge those beliefs, and the events in my life demand a still deeper understanding. More thought. More questions. More answers.

Ironically, as a college student, I took great pride walking around campus with Bertrand Russell's *Why I Am Not A Christian* under my arm. To be sure that no one missed my strong personal statement and to revel in other students' judgment, I made sure the cover was in clear sight of everyone as I walked to classes.

At that time, I think it was more the desire that people view me seriously as an intellectual than a statement of spiritual belief.

Years later when I once again read that powerful work, I understood how much I had missed because of my rush to be noticed. Russell actually struggles with the possible existence of a God, including the "first cause," "natural-law by design" and a variety of moral arguments. Each case is presented powerfully and he refuses to give the reader an easy answer. He concludes,

"Religion is based, I think, primarily and mainly upon fear. It is partly the terror of the unknown and partly, as I have said, the wish to feel that you have a kind of elder brother who will stand by you in all your troubles and disputes... A good world needs knowledge, kindliness, and courage; it does not need a regretful hankering after the past or a fettering of the free intelligence by the words uttered long ago by ignorant men."

Despite Russell's powerful words and undeniable logic, it only made me want to explore my own beliefs more. The journey has been a never-ending series of conclusions that seem only to open up new avenues of knowledge.

Who is this God and what is my relationship to such a deity?

Ironically, I'm someone who always loved ritual, especially old-fashioned gospel music.

Growing up we swayed to the traditional hymns sung by George Beverly Shea and Bill Monroe. When a great uncle died in the Seven Mountains, you could find the family at the end of the funeral around the piano in the parlor, singing our hearts out. Now, some nights I still find myself drifting to the *Gaither Television Homecoming Hour*. Only today, I love Signature Sound because they're hot, have great moves and still sing the old-fashioned hymns.

Despite my attraction to certain elements of organized religion, organized religion over the years found every conceivable opportunity to push me away. Only during the civil rights years in the 1960s—at the height of liberation theology—did I find myself pulled back into organized religion; but in truth, that only lasted awhile. As much as I wanted to belong, I found myself once again becoming more hostile to the negative impact that organized religion had on the world.

Clinching my distrust was the church response to the fight for LGBT rights and the early years of HIV/AIDS. More than ever, I desperately needed spirituality to help me come to terms with the epidemic. There never was a time in my life when a search for answers from a "higher power" was more important. As I lost nearly 300 friends to HIV/AIDS, I was seeking answers. Where did all this tragedy, sickness and societal hatred fit into my life? I wanted to pray. I wanted to lose myself in a place of unconditional love and support. Everyone around me was being drained by this holocaust and for so many of us, a spiritual answer was urgently needed.

This rocky journey has led to my spirituality today. For me, it is the combination of nature, sexuality, family, friends and the beauty of everyday life. Bringing joy into a world filled with hate, making people laugh, bonding with other men and creating my own rituals have made me look back on the journey with wonder. For me, God is life. Each day, I have been given the gift of life and I am thankful and grateful.

My Coming Out

Before I came out in 1976, I lied to everyone. Often I would be the first to laugh at "faggot jokes" and the last to come to someone's defense who was out. When I dared to get drunk or high enough to have sex, I would invent different personalities, names and bios so hopefully no one could figure out my real identity. While closeted I was blackmailed, almost committed suicide and did anything I could to prevent people from knowing I was a homosexual. Looking back on all those years where I lied, denied my very being and lived in shame and fear, I think, "What a waste."

But coming out was a rocky process. My mother and father responded with words to me that I never, ever thought they would use in relationship to their son. My sister Patsy frantically did her best to hold the entire situation together. My mother begged me

not to tell my brother and, to this day, I'm not quite sure why. In those initial years, going home was a place to avoid instead of a place of joy. Even after my family began to accept me, I was expected not to bring "it" up in front of them. I hated what this process was doing to me; I hated what it was doing to them.

When I came out, very few people with whom I worked with either professionally or politically supported that decision. Elected officials who I had worked side by side with for years suddenly wouldn't accept my calls or my checks. People stopped sending me invitations, and it was a very lonely time. As I was being rejected by most of my circle of support, I was totally new to the LGBT community and knew nothing about it. Eventually I worked my way to the gay Metropolitan Community Church and the Los Angeles Gay Center, which was a tiny organization back then. Slowly I found other members of the community who shared an interest in politics and cared for each other. Nevertheless, many of them weren't out to their families or at work.

In the midst of all this bleakness, one funny situation occurred after I heard of a small group in Los Angeles called the Stonewall Democratic Club. It made sense to me that I should go to a gathering where I could meet fellow Democrats who were gay. The Center directed me to their meeting in a Savings and Loan conference room. I put on a sharp blue suit, white shirt, tie and my best black shoes. Showing up at the meeting, I found nine people there. None of them talked to me, and I sat at the end of a table alone. Turns out they thought I was a cop sent to intimidate them because of the coat and tie!

The coming out process was horrible for me. My shame was overwhelming and I seriously considered—for a second time—

taking my life. These events led to a nervous breakdown; a collapse that took months to work through until I could get back on my feet.

Then a strange sensation started to come over me; the community got to know me and I was accepted. Never have I known such unconditional love and support. My image of them had been that they were not like me. I thought that they had had an easy time coming out. It made me realize that all of us had struggled and all of us wanted to be free. I discovered pride and was able to remove the shame.

Most importantly, my new friends and I made a pact that we would do whatever possible so that no future generation would have the pain of coming out that we had experienced. We would help make sure the LGBT community was a welcoming place. We'd operate from a place of love and not hate. Never again should any person feel pain in coming out.

Spring and Sexuality

With spring in bloom one can't help but think of sexuality as the animals around the woods are taking the new season to heart. They are breeding all over the place. It appears that the does have headed deep into the forest to find safe places to give birth to the little fawns. Soon my yard will be filled with baby deer and overly protective mothers. Sounds like a visit to some of my friends' houses.

It seems like every time I look out the window some animal is getting it on. The new spring must be an aphrodisiac, full of fragrant blossoms, warm afternoon sunshine, soft green grass and the music of a warm wind blowing through new leaves. I wish I could offer them privacy, but I must admit I am too curious to watch the various ways that animals express love and create life. I thought I was wise to the ways of the world, but these animals have positions, noises and techniques that make all of us look like squares.

Now, I wonder where they learned them. Is there a course provided by the adult animals for the young ones to learn the mating calls and the ABC's of mating? Or do the young ones instinctively know what is expected and what is available as they get older?

Sexuality is such a powerful force in all of our lives and as much pleasure as it gives us, it can also cause great pain. For most of us, sexuality was either spoken about in whispers or not at all. When I was growing up, there was no lecture from my parents, no sex education class in school and certainly no books in any library that would enable us to seek answers to why these strange urges were surfacing. We were left to fend for ourselves.

What little information we did get from institutions like churches, schools, the media and our families was laced heavily with fear and shame. No one urged us to reach inside ourselves to realize our fantasies and to discover the joy of fulfilling them. Never were we urged to use sexuality as a form of bonding, expression or self-discovery. People who deviated from the traditional missionary positions and engaged in role-play, experimented or simply make it a place of great joy were often held up to ridicule. Many of those who openly celebrated their sexuality were described as sick and often shunned by others.

Just think: if we as a society could lift some of that shame and replace it with joy and discovery. How many marriages have ended in divorce over sexual issues? How many people have gone through life in anger and feeling shame for having what, in reality, are harmless fantasies? How many expressions of love and joy have been left behind because of the fear of being viewed as sick or not normal?

Since my youth, we have come a long way. I think more and more parents are being responsible and having healthy conversations with their children about sexuality. People are starting to insist on the right to explore and stretch the bounds of what is viewed as "normal." There are publications for almost any fantasy or fetish, which does not leave one feeling alone or shame. Some schools have sex education classes.

Wouldn't it be wonderful if sex became a healing place that is filled with love, trust and adventure? That one could share experiences openly and with pride.

It seems to me that we need education not only on the physical aspects of sexuality but also the spirituality. We need to learn how to honestly conduct positive dialogue with our partners and to learn to respect not only their desires but also their emotions and feelings. We should work so that sexuality becomes a place of beauty and joy. We should work to become at one with nature with our sexuality and make it a spiritual journey of self-discovery.

One evening I was at a dinner party and a person at the table with great judgment in their voice said, "I hear they are disgusting and they act like animals in the bedroom." From what I can see outside my window, that might not be a bad thing.

The Woods

Last night it rained and I woke up to a green vision. Suddenly with the little rain, the forest around the house started to become lush. The trees had leaves and the firs were rapidly pushing up through the forest floor. Seeing the transformation from barren, stark, white winter to this blossoming that was like a miracle. We don't have spring in Turkey Hollow. In just a couple of weeks, we go—bang!—from barren to lush.

The forest throughout literature has always been home to hidden and enchanted places. No matter if it is the darkness of *Little Red Riding Hood* or Robin Hood's Sherwood, it all takes place in the deep forest. Thank God the stories didn't become mixed or we would have had the Wolf eating Little John. Seemed the deeper you go into the thickness of the growth, the more hidden treasures we found.

As a child, we were allowed at a very young age to walk across the fields into our woods. We always had to leave a note on the old icebox to let the folks know, "I am in the woods." Everyone knew where "the woods" were and knew where to find us. Being very short and young at the time, every tree looked like a California Redwood to me. Trees were great to scramble up and be a lookout for unwelcome intruders.

Just barely old enough to have minimal common sense, I would trek deeper in the forest, seeking its mysteries, looking for treasure and creating new hideouts. There was a stream roaring through our woods, and it was filled with tadpoles, frogs and other exotic finds. Trees fallen over the stream made for spanning tightropes like in a circus. Every once in a while, your navigation skills would fail and into the water you would go. I would make boats out of leaves and twigs and send them down the stream and marvel at how far they traveled.

In one location, full-bloomed honeysuckle vines had grown over fallen trees. Finding a passage into the "perfect hiding place" was not easy, but once one was created you suddenly had a fort with the incredible smell of honeysuckle. You were convinced no one would be able to find you, and you could do all sorts of wonderful boy-type stuff. In that massive canopy I dug holes and buried my most valuable things to protect them from the pirates, which usually consisted of my brother, Melvin, and his friends.

Even with sudden summer thunderstorms, my vine-created fort would stay remarkably dry—a lesson learned then that now helps me to understand where deer go during storms here in Turkey Hollow. Often returning across the fields of peas or tomatoes, I would be covered head to toe in mud. Mom wouldn't let me in our country house and I had to go under the weeping willow in the back of the house and turn on the spigot and wash myself cleaned. I think that is the first time I seriously considered becoming a nudist. There was something so magical about returning from the woods, being forced to wash off before entering the warm welcoming home—and being a "bad boy." I loved it.

Of course, every summer evening as we sat on the back porch with neighbors and family dropping by, Mom would recount with great amusement what a mess I looked like when I came back from the woods that day. I was so proud of my being the center of attention and was determined to be even more messy the next journey into the deep, dense, mysterious forest filled with great unknowns.

Time Out

The last couple of weeks have been extraordinarily busy with all sorts of activity—writing and the work that must be done to make repairs from winter and embrace summer. The first set of wildflowers pushed rapidly upwards after the heavy rains. By the end of the week, I was not, as Tennyson says, "that force which used to move heaven and earth."

So this weekend is a "time out" weekend. I have a great new friend visiting—we might be rocking on the porch with the rain beating down on my tin roof, turkeys and deer dancing among the new wildflowers and even a bobcat making a kill in my back yard. My friend and I may sit in front of the outdoor fire, sharing life stories and laughing a lot. What a special time.

Taking time out used to not be part of my life journey, having convinced myself that I was so important that my absence for even a weekend from the turmoil of the world would put the planet in jeopardy. How could everyone continue if I wasn't totally on top of things? Wouldn't I lose control of all that I had worked on so hard?

Imagine my surprise when because of sheer exhaustion I was forced to take some time off years ago. As I rested, I realized the planet was continuing to spin, traffic did not come to a screeching halt and my friends seemed to be doing just fine without my energy or input. Quite honestly, it was the most liberating of feelings. More importantly, when I was ready to once more put myself into the fray, I was rested, my mind was clear and new ideas flooded into my head. With that realization, I now know the urgency of everyone taking time off, to rest, renew and most importantly to find some joy and fun in their lives.

My momma used to say that if I didn't live my own life the way I wanted the world to be, then how would I be able to describe it to the world? It makes such sense, doesn't it? So now I am adamant about having joy, fun, sexuality and love in my life. How wonderful that I actually notice the wildflowers and wildlife. Or never forget the sunset a week ago or the one that my friend Steven Guy saw about six months ago. And I have time to read, listen to music and catch up on new films or see again classics like *All About Eve*. I love my time outs.

Gandhi used to call them his "wilderness years," when he instinctively knew that he needed to return home to spin, think and regain the purity of his soul. So I urge everyone to take a long weekend, devise a lovely vacation plan, see the world and come back to us with your personal gifts enhanced and your being more valuable to us all.

The Day Dr. King Died

One of the aspects I love about living in Turkey Hollow is that it is often so removed from the harshness of the world. When the spring sun is out, the deer are grazing and the air is clean, the ugliness of the outside world seems so far away. The key debate around here isn't politics or religion, but the weather because that will determine the navigability of our dirt road. Yet, sometimes the reality of the world seeps in and we're forced to live not only current events but also relive those that changed the world forever.

When I read this week that it has been forty years since Dr. Martin Luther King, Jr. was killed, it took my breath away. How could so much time pass so quickly? The events of that day and, in fact, that year, are entrenched into my mind as if they occurred yesterday. How do you explain that terrible year when Dr. King and Senator Kennedy were assassinated to a youngster? The horrors of those moments and the images never leave. The sense of emptiness you still feel every time you hear their names evoked. Did we really live through such a year or was it all a nightmare?

In April of 1968, I was a young twenty-year-old man. The first three months of that year I had traveled from one end of the country to the other organizing for Senator Eugene McCarthy, a peace candidate for president of the United States. Thousands and thousands of young students were filled with idealism and hope. We were winning the battle against the Vietnam War, and we had just forced President Lyndon Johnson not to seek reelection. Everything, it seemed, was going our way.

On the fourth of that month, I was headed from the national campaign headquarters for McCarthy in Washington to Philadelphia to work on the Pennsylvania primary. My orders were to stop briefly in the city of Brotherly Love and immediately catch a plane to Pittsburgh, where I would help organize the field operations for the peace candidates. As I departed the train in 30th Street station in Philly and entered the main room, I noticed a huge crowd gathered around a flickering black and white television monitor. Women were on their knees praying and some men were muttering angrily. I couldn't quite figure out what was wrong. Then an elderly African American man, who looked gentle and kind, looked at me with cold, steely eyes and said, "Y'all finally killed him." Puzzled, I asked, "Killed who?" With tears in his eyes he answered, "Dr. King."

The wind was taken totally out of me, and I fell onto one of the station's long wooden benches. Out of breath, I just stared at him and finally started sobbing. The elderly man suddenly transformed and sat next to me and put his arm around me, saying over and over, "I know, son. I know." I cried into his shoulder as he held me. I simply could not believe that "they" had killed one of two men who had shaped my politics. The first, John Kennedy, was also killed by a bullet less than five years earlier. How could this happen in America? How?

Not knowing what to do, I pulled myself together and attempted to apologize to the elderly man and also to thank him for his kindness all at the same time. He patted me on the shoulder and just walked away into his own sorrow and grief. Even in death, Dr. King brought us briefly together. None of us were alone that day.

May I Have This Dance?

This week when I was in Peck's Country Store, I noticed on the public bulletin board a lot of ads placed by young women selling last year's prom dresses for a steal to this year's crop of young prom queens. I smiled as I remembered all the ways that dance has impacted my life.

When I was in Woodstown High School, we used to have Friday night canteens (dances). Interestingly, in the early-1960s African-Americans would still dance on one side of the gym while whites danced on the other. There were no mandatory rules requiring the separation, but it was just the way things were back then.

My senior prom date was Patricia Miller who looked stunning in her full white dress and the gardenia wrist corsage I gave her. I was every bit the gentlemen (and also very closeted) and the most memorable part of the evening for me was almost falling asleep on the way home and driving off the road.

As I started going to gay bars in my twenties, I was very reluctant to dance with a man. Somehow I had the absurd notion that dancing with another man would make me "more gay." Finally, I couldn't resist the beat of Donna Summer, Diana Ross and Thelma Houston, and I hit the dance floor with my best dancing moves. Now, I don't think I would qualify for *So You Think You Can Dance* but I had some great moves; well-timed twists and swirls, the music moved through me. Travolta and Swayze would have been impressed as I bopped around to "Love to Love You Baby"

To dance one's ass off in the gay disco's of the seventies was one thing, but it was totally another to slow dance with a man. The thought was really too much for me. My barrier broke down in a little bar called One in the San Fernando Valley in Southern California. The bar was divided into two sections, a disco and an intimate cabaret piano bar. I was drawn to the group singing "There's a Place for Us" gathered around the piano to begin the evening. Then eventually I was beckoned to the dance floor to display my free spirited moves.

One night the DJ played "There's a Place for Us" and the guys started slow dancing. I immediately hit the sidelines and watched in amazement. Then this masculine vision dressed head to toe in Levi walked over and simply said, "May I have this dance?" I was dumbfounded as he guided me out to the floor. Thank God he had the good sense to let me lead. In the middle of the dance, he put his head on my shoulder, and we both sighed. I was in sheer heaven having this wonderful freedom of intimacy with this handsome man. The young man's name was Paul and he was a horse trainer. We danced all night, and I felt free and alive.

Many years later in 1992, I had to face yet one more barrier that dealt with dance. After a very successful year assisting Bill Clinton getting elected to the Presidency, I scored the best tickets to 1993 Presidential Inaugural Ball. The National Ball was to be held at the National Museum Building in Washington, D.C. My date was David Davis, a handsome man who is also a very good friend. I was absolutely determined to dance at my first Inaugural Ball. Now, as silly as it may seem today, this was a major deal back fifteen years ago. My gay friends begged me not to make a "spectacle" of myself and warned that two men slow dancing at the Ball would be fodder for the sensationalist press.

I agonized about it for days leading up to the Ball. Much to his credit, my date David was quite comfortable either way. He just wanted to be supportive of me. Finally, the evening arrived and the slow music started. I turned to David and said, "May I have this dance?" He smiled and we glided to the floor. Much to our surprise, the other dancers moved away from us and left us dancing alone. I have never felt so awkward. Suddenly a very elderly couple came out of the sidelines and moved right next to us and smiled. The elderly women said to us, "We always like to dance next to the best dancers." Having broken the ice, the other dancers on the floor closed in around us and the rest is history.

Turkeys Come Home

Like the swallows returning to Capistrano, the turkeys have returned to Turkey Hollow.

Now the hills around here are filled with wild turkeys but none have chosen to take up residence in my "back four," otherwise known to city folk as the back four acres. Clearly the deer have shared with turkeys "Franklin" and "Eleanor" what a good gig they have found in the woods just off our clearing. The noble birds have made a home in a large pile of fallen trees that were toppled from this winter's Northeasters. To add a comfy touch, the tree trunks are covered with hanging vines.

So the two turkeys have obviously realized that they have found not only a good Democratic household but also one with plenty of surprise treats. I can almost hear them gobble-gobble around the clock. At times the sounds seem strangely erotic, and

I turn my heads away from where they have made home. Even turkeys have a right to privacy in such moments. The wood and vines not only give them comfort but also protects their nest from predators.

Eleanor and Franklin have reason to be worried. Because as mud season ends and temperatures hit near eighty degrees, we are getting a census of who will be our summer guests from the animal kingdom. Foremost among them is a stunning hawk—clearly a Republican—that swoops down to snatch eggs and small prey with no concern for anyone except himself. "Bush" Hawk's appearance is so powerful you can't imagine he wouldn't use his power to help others. But no, alas, his only intention is to make life miserable for our fellow residents like Eleanor and Franklin. My little cats definitely are not going outside while Bush rules the skies.

The deer that no longer have to search frantically for food as in the harsh snow-covered months are in heaven eating everything in sight. The pregnant does are starting to look for places deep in the forest where they safely can give birth. Soon we will have little fawns barely able to walk challenging others for turf. On the other hand, our yearlings and proud bucks are enjoying the absence of the does and seem to be having a bachelor party in our clearing.

Since the deer pig-out on anything that has color and a vine, only the daffodils, which have started to bloom, give hints of color in this busy crossroads of wild life. For some reason the small yellow bloom has developed its own defenses from the scavenging deer. Matching the bold yellow house, they defiantly insist that this isn't all a drab sepia-colored operation.

Finally, this week, high in the sky was the boss of it all—the American Bald Eagle. Making a great comeback across the nation, it flew higher than the rest, glided across its kingdom, observing everything in sight and comfortable in the knowledge that he alone has been crowned our national emblem.

Now all we have left is for Benny the Bear to make his appearance and see how he held up during his winter hibernation. Once again it is time to make sure those cans are in the garage and no fruit is left on the screen porch. After all, who in this stunningly beautiful weather wants to end up on the back porch banging pans to remind Benny of his boundaries?

Twenty Years and Counting

As the rain fell hard on the tin roof of my screened porch this week, I couldn't help but reflect upon the twentieth anniversary of my parter Peter Scott's death. Incessant rain on a tin roof demands that you take time for reflection. At first, I insisted to myself that the anniversary of the death of a man I loved deeply was just a date on the calendar and that one must move on. Then I realized that in many ways, Peter's death was a symbol of a nightmare era of vast devastation and horror from HIV/AIDS. And although all these years have passed, the images, the sorrow and the disbelief feel like yesterday.

Twenty years ago this past Wednesday, friends and loved ones gathered around Peter's bed. Those of us who loved and cared for him for three years had hoped against hope that this strong, handsome, brilliant son of a West Texas ranching family would be one of the exceptions and survive the plague. Peter was in ecstasy when I would massage his big ol' feet at the end of the bed. He would often laugh, even in good times, and beg me never to stop. In his final hours, I held his feet in my hands, gently rubbing them, tears streaming down my face and me begging God not to take this young man from me. He struggled for breath, and we told him it was time to make the transition. Peter had been in such pain and was so very sick. At this stage, we just wanted him to be free and to once again know peace—this time outside his body.

For nearly a decade, I repeated that ritual; standing next to countless bedsides of young men under forty as they gasped for survival. My job at those moments was to help the survivors find the strength to honor their dead and to return to life once again. One young man after another seemed to disappear from us weekly and sometimes daily. Each intimate moment of making the transition had its own uniqueness, brought new tears and intensified the bafflement as to why this was happening to gay people. Adding to the burden was the fact that the insurance companies wouldn't cover us, people stopped inviting us to dinner, the government fought us instead of easing our pain and even undertakers often wouldn't bury us. The unbelievable horror of mass death was made worse by the intense discrimination and total indifference toward our plight. Because of my background as a public speaker, I would frequently be asked to eulogize the departed. Saturdays came to mean yet one more funeral and the struggle to find unique words to capture each young warrior's death.

However that May 13th was different. Peter was dying. I simply couldn't imagine my life without him. For over a decade we had endured each other's best and worst. Every aspect of our lives was interwoven into a fabric that just didn't seem to be able to exist without the other. That day, my strength came from my community helping me heal as I had helped so many others. Never have I seen such courage, nobility and determination to care for the sick and dying. The story of the LGBT community during this horrible decade is one that should be the source of poetry, art, songs and stories for years to come. We must never forget.

Even today when someone rubs my feet, I tense a little as Peter's last moments flash into my head. Sometimes driving down the road, I do a double take as I see someone who looks just like him. My life is filled with gifts, friends, laughter and success after twenty years. Yet my soul and heart will never forget that day, those times and the man, who, like so many friends, disappeared into the night.

Kate and Pete

All spring, I have written about the weather and animals of Turkey Hollow, just like one of my favorite writers Henry David Thoreau. After my piece about sexuality among the animals, some of my friends were concerned that I was less Thoreau and more Dr. Doolittle. I received calls from some, asking, "Just how often do you 'talk' to these animals in the backyard?" and "Don't you think it is time to come down off that mountain top and maybe take a long vacation among people?"

Fear not, I live in a vibrant community with wonderful neighbors and a great history. Just this week, *The Sullivan County Democrat* reported that in 1897, Joseph O'Keefe was hoeing his father's field when he was kicked by a mule and died on the spot. The paper wrote of the outpouring from neighbors who responded to the O'Keefe family's grief. On a more joyful note, the paper also reported that in the same year, young John Malloy had the honor of raising the flag at President Grant's Tomb in New York and how proud the entire area was of that achievement.

Since mules have disappeared from Turkey Hollow and Grant's Tomb isn't as notable, those of us up here on the mountain have to depend on the summer crowd to bring us stories and a bit of civilization. However, the summer crowd is increasingly overshadowed by year around weekend residents from New York City. Sullivan County is filled with second homes dotted across the hilltops and deep in the valley.

Even though most come up on weekends, Memorial Day is still the official kick-off of the entertaining season. It is when your home officially becomes a bed and breakfast for tons of friends who suddenly discover your existence in the cold North, finally warmed by spring. Also it is a time for those coveted invitations to the more beautiful homes whose residents will hold exciting and special gatherings.

For me, an invitation to Kate and Pete's home is the most exciting.

Kate and Pete are a young couple, both with stunning good looks, and they are so kind and intelligent. Kate and Pete seem to be hopelessly in love with each other. They remind me of a young Tracy and Hepburn or Newman and Woodward. They don't miss life and seem to enjoy every second of it. Most importantly, they are spectacular at creating moments of beauty at their home on the mountaintop.

The other night I was invited to Kate's birthday, and it captured perfectly what is so special about an evening at their place. You drive up a long drive to the top of their hill greeted by a quaint French Normandy-type home and a huge meadow overlooking the valley. Kate, who is an incredible cook, prepared a delicious meal with the help of her mother and a few friends. We sat outside, taking in the evening, enjoying the stunning mountain views. Kate seemed to particularly glow that evening as the sunset captured her beautiful blond locks. Pete, who is a handsome man's man, was so happy to be celebrating Kate's birthday.

Quite honestly, all evening all I could think about was Danish Baroness Karen von Blixen-Finecke (Isak Dinesen) in *Out of Africa*. Kate had been playing ancient records on an old Victrola by the picnic table, giving us the Andrews Sisters' "Apple Blossom Time." She had to wind the handle on the side to play the next record. You could imagine Redford and Streep dancing on the hill.

As dinner finished, Pete, along with his best buddy Michael, headed to the meadow to build a huge old-fashioned bonfire. No one makes bonfires like Pete. He is an artist at it. Michael was the perfect assistant, and they seemed like tribal warriors gathering wood for the clan. We left the picnic table after the sun had gone to rest and headed to sit around the huge fire for coffee and an incredible homemade dessert. The fire blazed furiously and the stars matched its glory.

As great conversation took place around the warmth of the fire into the chill of the night, I sat back in my chair, and with a big smile, said to myself, "It just doesn't get any better than this."

Not only has the wildlife brought me joy in Turkey Hollow, so have Kate and Peter.

So you all can relax, I am in still in civilization even though the soundtrack is on a Victrola playing the Andrews Sisters.

San Francisco

My friend Steven and I left the burgeoning wildlife population of Turkey Hollow to head to San Francisco. Now that is not an easy trip. We have to make sure everything is set right for the animals before we leave, then drive three hours to the nearest airport, which is followed by a six hour flight across country. Can't wait for there to be a Turkey Hollow International Airport.

The reason for our trek west was I was being honored by GLAAD with their "Pioneer in Media Award," a distinction that greatly humbles me. GLAAD, which is clearly one of the foremost LGBT organizations in the country, has achieved new vitality under the leadership of former Tempe Arizona mayor Neil Giuliano. So having this potent and powerful media watchdog committee recognize me for my writings and years of activism is overwhelming.

Coming to San Francisco for the big dinner caused a flood of memories, reminding me of all that is special about this historic city.

My first trip to the City by the Bay was when I was a student at Arizona State University during the height of the Haight-Ashbury days and the infamous "Summer of Love" in 1967. The Haight was the center of the new hippie movement and source of most of the great music of the 1960s. I remember going to a concert in Golden Gate Park organized against the Vietnam War. My friends and I took acid and danced with each other in the rampant greenery as the throng joined together as one. I had purchased prism glasses to distort everything, and I thought I was the coolest guy in the park.

Later as an organizer against the Vietnam War, I returned to the city to help prepare for the massive marches in 1969. For this trip, however, the drugs were put away; we were entirely caught up in the struggle against this horrible war. San Francisco has always done its own thing, and for any outsiders to pretend that they could organize the city was just ludicrous. Organizing out of D.C., the most we could hope for was that our events could be coordinated to operate on the same day.

In the spring of 1976, I moved to the Castro district of San Francisco. I was just coming out of the closet and like most homosexuals headed from the interior to the Coasts. Everyone was going to the "Mecca by the Bay," where we could be free and celebrate being gay. It was such a wonderful time of sexual freedom and experimentation. Free from all those suffocating years in closet, for six glorious months I was able to catch up for lost time. My euphoria was interrupted when Mayor Tom Bradley asked me to come to Los Angeles to run his re-election campaign. Although sad to leave my new home, I gratefully accepted.

In 1984, the city hosted the Democratic Convention and I returned as Co-chair of the California delegation, which was firmly in the hands of young charismatic reformer Senator Gary Hart from Colorado. Without a doubt, of the nine national conventions that I have attended, it remains one of my favorites. The highlight for me was being able to vote for the first woman ever to be on a national ticket, Congresswoman Geraldine Ferraro. It was at that convention that my niece saw me on television standing on a chair chanting, "You gotta have Hart!" She turned to her mother and said, "Look at crazy Uncle David misbehaving."

In 1978, working with Supervisor Harvey Milk, I helped defeat the notorious Briggs Initiative in California. Shockingly, not long afterwards, the passionate Milk, along with Mayor George Moscone, was assassinated by fellow Supervisor Dan White. San Francisco was suddenly a place of candles and tears.

It was a grim patina that would continue through the 1980s. For almost the next eight years, my visits to the beautiful city were clouded by misery and gloom. Trips were to coordinate our battle against HIV/AIDS, to attend funerals or to demonstrate for healthcare. Every visit reminded me of someone who was no longer alive. Sadness and death was everywhere.

My return in 1991 was a happier event; in the Oak Room of the Clift Hotel, I convinced Supervisor Roberta Achtenberg to be the first elected official in California to endorse a young Arkansas Governor named Bill Clinton. She become Co-chair of his campaign in California and later went on to be the highest openly LGBT person serving in his administration.

Over the years, the City by the Bay has become a place of dear friends, fond memories and spectacular beauty. It will always have a special place in my heart.

No on 6 and Ronald Reagan

Ever since the movie *Milk* was released, I have been asked questions about the "No on Proposition 6" campaign in 1978. Harvey Milk was basically the leader in Northern California and the statewide operation was run out of the Southern California office. Ivy Bottini was Harvey's counterpart in the grassroots operation in the south. Two straight politicos, Don Bradley and Mike Levitt, along with Peter Scott and I, worked on the fundraising, the press, the media campaign and so forth.

We had a great relationship with Harvey and his team. We worked closely and in coordination. I guess the best evidence of that was that David Goodstein of *The Advocate* hated us all. He never even wanted to fight back against Proposition 6; his solution was to just take it to court. That was totally unacceptable to all of us both in the north and the south and that solidarity helped us bond together.

Despite all our good work, everyone involved had taken the proposition from 75% in favor of firing homosexual schoolteachers down to only 55%. We were having a helluva a time gaining that last 6%. We knew we needed something big to push us over the top, and we needed it soon, since we were in the last weeks of the campaign.

There is no doubt in my mind that the man who put us over the top was California Governor Ronald Reagan. His opposition to Proposition 6 killed it for sure. In my book *Stranger Among Friends*, I tell the story of the Reagan endorsement. Here is an excerpt:

The gap in the polls kept on narrowing. Victory seemed more and more likely. Still, there is nothing in politics more dangerous than over confidence. We decided we needed a campaign bombshell to put us over the top. One day Peter (Scott) and I had a call from a closeted homosexual, Don Livingston, a senior executive with the Carter, Hawley, Hale Department stores who asked us: "Would the endorsement of Ronald Reagan be helpful?" Would it! Previously, Don had been a member of Governor Reagan's administrative staff, and he thought through his contacts there was a fair chance of obtaining this endorsement. Because Reagan was beginning to plan his run for the presidency, any effort to reach him had to be conducted in total secrecy, and Don was our liaison in setting up a confidential meeting between a member of the governor's staff and Peter and me.

We met at a Denny's in Hispanic East Los Angeles—about as safe a place as we could conceive, since the likelihood of a

Republican showing up there seem minimal. The staffer, too, was a closeted homosexual, but he ended up confident that he could trust us not to reveal this and that we would make a good impression on the Governor. He agreed to arrange a meeting.

When the time came he warned us that we we'd have only a few minutes to make our case. He urged that we stick to libertarian principles. He reminded us that there were many on Reagan's staff opposed to the meeting, and it was the Governor himself that made the final determination to see us. The staffer felt that Nancy Reagan, who had many gay friends, would play a part in his decision on the initiative. Rarely have I been more on tenterhooks.

Peter and I were escorted into a bright office with windows overlooking West Los Angeles. Reagan rose from his desk, gave us his famous smile, extended his hand and said, "How nice of you boys to come over to chat with me about this issue."

He made us feel more at home than most Democrats did. He directed us to chairs and offered us soda. It was hard to believe that this smiling gentle man was the same person who had sent in three thousand bayoneted National Guardsmen to "protect" People's Park in Berkeley.

He opened the discussion. "I understand you boys have a case you want to make to me," he said.

"Governor, you know about the initiative that would allow any school child to file a complaint against any teacher that he thought was homosexual." I began. "This initiative would create anarchy in the classroom. Any child who received a failing grade or was disciplined by a teacher could accuse that teacher of being a homosexual. Teachers will become afraid of giving low grades or maintaining order in their classrooms."

We could see a surprised look come over Reagan's face. I think he expected to hear a human rights argument. "I never thought about that. It really could happen, couldn't it?"

"Governor, the kids control the classroom." Peter said, "Teachers are terrified of their students. It will be chaos."

"You mean, any accusation by a student must be heard by the school board?"

I knew we were making progress. "Exactly," I answered. "The law requires a public hearing before the local school board to decide if there are grounds for the charges or not. Each school district's school board meetings will become a circus."

Reagan smiled at us. "This might be a good day for you boys. Don't think we can allow something like that to happen here in California."

Clearly our argument was having an impact. He asked a number of questions about the wording of the initiative. He seemed to be well informed, and he spent a lot of time discussing the details. While he officially refused to tell us that he would oppose it, we left the meeting with very little doubt. He stood up, shook our hands, patted us on the back, and said, "Thanks, boys, for coming to see me. You are fine young lads. Your parents must be proud."

When we came out of the office, Reagan's staff cornered us and made it very clear that if word leaked about the meeting and if we didn't keep silent about the Governor's apparent support, our efforts could be derailed. We were on cloud nine when we got back to headquarters but we kept our mouths shut. We held numerous private phone conversations with the Reagan staff on wording and background information. At last, in a mid-September newspaper column, future president Ronald Reagan called for the defeat of Proposition 6, citing "the mischief" it could cause between students and teachers in the classroom. The column became front-page news all over California and the polls showed a strong shift against the initiative.

And that is the story of Ronald Reagan and Proposition 6. When election night rolled around we defeated it by over a million votes, carried even Orange County, and Anita Bryant was sent packing.

Quiet of the Hollow

Returning from a whirlwind trip to San Francisco and Washington, D.C., I was thrilled to be back in the quiet of the Hollow.

A gentle May rain greeted my return, feeding the vivid green forests that now dominate the Turkey Hollow. The chartreuse firs are rising, creating a colorful green carpet as far as the eye can see. The once expansive barren views of winter are now bountiful with brilliant colors. Landscapes remain protected until next fall's leaves begin to drift downward. Deer that used to be visible as they wandered down from the peak now can have their privacy until they arrive at the clearing behind the house.

What most strikes me every time I return home is the quiet.

Now don't confuse quiet with lack of activity. The forest is alive. Turkey Hollow this year is filled with activity greater than last spring. We have a pair of Wild Turkeys making a home in the "back four." Two Broad-winged Hawks have also been hanging about. I consulted with avid birder Ken Allaire who knows a thing or two about our feathered friends. The hawks are rather uncommon in these necks of the woods. They love to spend their winters in Panama at one of those new bird resorts. They often travel in groups of thousands during their migration. So we are thrilled to have them as honored guests. The Bald Eagles seem to be plentiful this year and soaring overhead all the time. Also, a little chickadee has made a nest on the front porch, dutifully tending to her eggs. We are about to have babies.

While the sounds of birds chirping at dawn and sunset are most pleasant music, they have nothing on the damn woodpeckers. These fancy colored birds demand total attention at dawn, usually right outside the bedroom window, as they peck away so loudly that it echo's throughout the Hollow. Sleeping late at this time of the year is out of the question. It appears that a group of woodpeckers are making a home out of the tree just outside my bedroom window.

Not to be outdone by our winged beauties, Benny the Bear made a dramatic return to the Hollow this week. Now this huge 300-pound plus Black Bear has been a fixture since last summer. Old Man Keller says they roam up to twenty-five miles and that we will only see him now and then. Wayne continues that once they pick an area we are most likely their new home. He has seen Benny the Bear up on his porch getting the honey from the hummingbird feeder.

Now, Benny wasn't content to just roam across the backyard making his presence known. He had to make sure he declared his

territory. For over an hour, he lay down scratched against a tree, playfully rolled about and explored every nook and cranny of the yard. Of course, my face was plastered against the window, sipping my morning coffee, watching in both awe and a little bit of fear. According to Wikipedia, these mammoth beasts can bring down little fawns and have them for dinner. Now the fawns are about to be born in the next weeks in Turkey Hollow and I want Benny to move on to his next favorite location. He has entertained me, given great photographs and announced his return. Time for him to move on.

The deer, of course, are eating like there is no tomorrow. After just making it through winter without starving, they are feasting on the abundant foliage. For them, this time of year is like a Swedish smorgasbord with endless choices of food. The does have retreated deep into the woods to prepare to give birth to this years crop of newborns. The appearance of these dainty beautiful creatures is actually the highlight of my year in Turkey Hollow. Shouldn't be too long before they make their debut.

In the meantime, I can laze in my rocking chair, sip coffee and take in the quiet, busy symphony of nature. The hills are alive with the sound of music.

Alice Roosevelt Longworth, the Artichoke and Me

Growing up in rural and isolated America in the 1950s didn't give you much chance to learn all the intricacies of good manners. Yet, my mom was a stickler for them and often said my sister and brother and I would someday be grateful to her. She made us write hand-written thank you notes and stand up if a lady came into the room. Mom desperately wanted us all to escape into a better life and was determined that she would at least provide the foundation.

We sometimes didn't have enough money to meet even our basic needs yet a copy of *Emily Post* sat on a shelf. That book symbolized my mom's hope that we would meet "fine people" and be invited into their homes. When times were very tight, that was not an excuse for bad manners. If we wanted to get out into the world, we had to know the rules and abide by them. No elbows on the table and don't you dare pick up the soup and drink from the bowl no matter if you were in a hurry to finish dinner.

My first real crisis in the manners department came in 1969 in Washington, D.C. Up to that point I had always been a young organizer who wore Levi's, a blue work shirt, a denim jacket, and cowboy boots topped off with my cowboy hat. That outfit (kind of sexy back then) served me well in living out that persona. As a result, cute David was never challenged in a serious way about his manners and "fine people." There was no question that I adhered to the basics of opening car doors, standing for elders and taking off my hat in front of ladies.

Then in the dining room of Secretary of Defense Robert McNamara, I met the artichoke. You wouldn't think that a simple artichoke would be the source of my potential downfall. However, it caused me to break out into a cold sweat. The McNamaras were famous for their Sunday morning brunches where the elite of Washington would gather to discuss world issues. Despite being one of the leaders of the anti-war protests at that time, being a friend of their daughter Kathy warranted me an invitation.

As I approached the table there were more knives and forks than they had in all the Russian Army. There were also enough glasses at each place setting to hold any possible liquid that would ever be put in a container. In the middle of it all sat that fucking artichoke, staring at me like it was my sworn enemy. Determined to take me down and humiliate me in front of all these powerful people. Trust me, I had no idea what the prickly, green, ugly thing on my plate was—never in my life had I seen one. Surely we weren't going to eat that tough, rubbery, sad excuse for a vegetable. My first thought was that some decorator thought it would make a nice decoration for the table

Sitting down, I just stared at the green monster. Next to me the McNamaras had placed Alice Roosevelt Longworth. She was the daughter of President Teddy Roosevelt and had married the Speaker of the House, who now has a Congressional office building named after him. Mrs. Longworth had cut quite a swath through society but now was at the pinnacle of it as the most sought after guest in the nation's capitol. She had a needlepoint pillow that read, "If you don't have anything good to say about someone, then please sit next to me." She was feisty and her one-liners were—and still are—legendary.

Seeing me immobilized by the artichoke, she leaned over and whispered, "You have no idea what that is, do you?"

"No, Mrs. Longworth," I murmured, "I do not." She patted my leg, smiled and said, "Just watch and follow me. I have no idea why they serve these damn things, but here we are." And with grace she tackled the artichoke as if it was her best friend. As she proceeded slowly, I followed step by step, doing my mom proud. Mrs. Longworth, who hated the Vietnam War, knew of my anti-war activities. At the end of the meal my new tutor gave me her number. With several visits to her famous home, she schooled me in D.C. social graces. At least she did to the best of her ability given that she had a real challenge in me.

For years I loved her for rescuing me from the artichoke.

Summer

Summer Memories

As the first day of June arrives, the general consensus here is that May was one of the coldest in quite some time. The sky spit down the last hours of snow just about mid-month, much to everyone's dismay.

So it is with arms open to the newly clear sunny sky that I welcome summer. Nearly overnight, the drab mid-season mud has become a forest of vivid greens. Dotted on top of well-watered fauna are white, orange, purple and blue wildflower blossoms. I can hear wildlife prancing invisibly behind a green forest curtain, until they are ready to step into the spotlight of the clearing. This wonderful spring, the adage has evolved into "May showers bring June flowers," and I finally have the chance to drink in all the incredible beauty of a new season in the country.

At night as I sit on the huge screened porch at twilight and watch the sun drop over the hills, I can't help but reminiscence about my childhood summers in Elmer, New Jersey.

It's impossible to count how often the family gathered on the porch, in the perfect stillness of glowing sunsets, and partook in the family tradition of telling stories. Passed down from generation to generation, storytelling was an art in my family. My Grandpa "Buzzard Bait" Grove would regale us of stories from the Seven Mountains. Now, in my youth, I believed every word Grandpa Grove had to say and never could figure out why his tales would solicit guffaws from all the adults. After all, I knew this masculine, cigar-puffing, big man in bib overalls, was capable of any feat he spoke of. He could barely write his own name but he alone was a poet of spinning tales of "good ol' times" and family lore. No one was more captivating than ol' Buzzard Bait.

As the sun went down in the evening, my brother and sister and I would set out to capture glowing lighting bugs that had emerged in the fields. I made certain to line the bottom of my jar with grass, as to make my brilliant prisoner more comfortable. The warm summer nights elicited laughter and joy as we ran creating our lanterns of nature. As far as the eye could see, the fields were mysteriously lit by the floating bugs to awesome effect. Mom would always insist that we release our captives at the end of the evening so the magic could continue.

Often we would eat outside on the porch. Sometimes Dad came home early from working Mr. Seabrook's farm and Mom had the day off so the night would be a special evening. My family lived off the land and summer evening meals featured baked stuffed tomatoes, potato salad, corn on the cob, fresh-shelled peas and homemade ice cream with strawberries from our garden. With no air conditioning in those days, the cool porch was the center of our universe after the scorching days. Late in the afternoon, we would hose down the heated porch boards to freshen up our nightly gathering spot.

Nature never failed to entertain on those summer evenings. If the lighting bugs were scarce, we would know that a storm was on the way. Since we could see across the flat fields of crops, the storms would always announce their arrival long before reaching us. My family and I would watch the western night skies become jagged with lighting strikes hitting the ground, knowing soon the storm would be right over us. There was such a strong anticipation of how violent and glorious the thunderstorms would be by the time they reached us. Often we would have to run into the house when the shady trees surrounding our land would draw a strike. None of us were eager to prove Ben Franklin's theories.

Then it would be off to bed. I had old bunk beds that my dad got from Seabrook Farms. They were first used by German prisoners during World War II, who were sent to work the farms during the War. I'm not sure if it is because they were caught in proximity of the United States or if they were brought over to assist in the labor shortage. The ones in Seabrook worked the farms as laborers. The metal beds with their thin mattresses could easily be used as a jungle gym and I loved them. I had them to myself and with the big wide windows open in my bedroom, the sounds of the crickets would sing me to sleep.

Sitting on my porch in Turkey Hollow, I have to laugh: look who's become Buzzard Bait.

Bobby

People in Turkey Hollow never forget those who have passed on. In the barbershop, the locals will talk of old friends and their kindnesses, regale with tales about what a great hunter they were or lovingly describe some very funny exploits. They remember past neighbors with great fondness; good folks are never forgotten no matter how long ago they walked among us.

This week the *New York Times* had a story on the anniversary of Senator Robert Kennedy's death. It was a moving tribute and caused my friends and I to exchange emails about where we were that day and the period of mourning that followed. None of us had any problem remembering; it still made us extremely sad as we recalled this once in a lifetime man. While he was a distinguished senator, a candidate for president and a legend around the world, the people only knew him as "Bobby."

That fateful day in June I was in California with the Senator Eugene McCarthy team having just finished a tough and at times bitter California primary. Senator Kennedy was winning it decisively and it appeared he was on the way to the nomination. It was a disappointing loss for the McCarthy campaign after so much work but most of us were also passionate about Bobby.

Up watching the late returns that showed the landslide for Kennedy narrowing, I sat in my hotel room stunned as a special report suddenly interrupted, announcing that he had been shot in the kitchen of the Ambassador Hotel in Los Angeles. After having gone through the assassinations of President Kennedy and Dr. Martin Luther King, Jr. all any of us could do was scream, "No, no, no!" and break down in sobs. All over the Beverly Wilshire Hotel you could hear similar cries filling the dark night sky. People grabbed phones and called loved ones. Shaking, I phoned my sister Patsy in Baltimore where it was in the early morning hours and could only shout into the receiver, "They shot him! They shot him!" She knew instantly who had been shot. By that time, it seemed the world needed our nation to suffer one more assassination that would change the direction of the planet forever.

All I wanted to do was to get back to Washington and catch a train to my sister's house in Baltimore. This one was just too overwhelming and any thoughts of what was next just didn't seem to have room in either my head or heart. I arrived in Baltimore exhausted, and like the rest of the nation, I was glued to the television set watching the funeral in St. Patrick's Cathedral in New York City. There were moments you never forget from that service such as Senator Ted Kennedy's eulogy or Andy Williams singing the "Battle Hymn of the Republic."

Then began the long train ride from New York to Washington, D.C. Millions, literally millions, lined the tracks between these two cities. My sister had political connections and we were able to get on the platform at the station in Baltimore to watch the funeral train pass. We waited for hours since the train had to go so very slowly because of the crowds. While waiting we shared stories of where we had been when we heard the terrible news. Then we began singing freedom songs with thousands and thousands joining in.

Slowly the locomotive appeared and we suddenly—without prompting—held hands and started singing "We Shall Overcome" as the train traveled through the station. The flag-draped coffin hit our hearts and once it passed we all cried our eyes out. We walked home in silence, knowing that the world had changed with just a bullet. Never again in the campaign was there such energy or spirit. So much hope had died with Bobby; his death had robbed us as a nation one more time. One crazy man with a gun had taken it all away from us. We continued working though the campaign but it was a joyless exercise, like putting one foot in front of the other. The horror of the Chicago Convention that summer with the troops and police beating the peace protesters seemed just like a logical extension from the horror of Bobby's death.

Like the good ones up here in Turkey Hollow, Bobby will never be forgotten. Stories of his courage, his humor, his compassion and his family will linger with us forever.

Hustle and Bustle

For such a remote place, Turkey Hollow sure has been bustling with activity. It is also the time of year you have all these great plans and as each summer day passes, one item drops from your "things to do" list.

On the eve of every summer, I'm determined to go back to the days of my youth when we sun-dried the bed sheets on the outside clothesline. If you have never had sheets dried in the sun, then you don't know what you are missing. The smell of fresh bedding is just unbelievable. Of course, I get all nostalgic until I remember what was involved. Back in rural New Jersey, our first washer was on four legs and had an open top capped by a hand wringer. We had to put the sheets in the ancient machine, and it would "agitate" the linens with soap. Next, the sheets had to go through the wringer into a big tub of clear water where they would then be rinsed by hand. Finally, for good measure, we would put them through the hand wringer one more time and then carry a heavy basket of wet percales out into the yard to hang them on the clothes line as the winds came howling across the pea fields. Luck would have to be on your side as a young child not to drop one on the ground—because then the entire process would have to be repeated. Upon reflection, I think I will just once more stuff them into a pillow case and take them to be professionally washed, pressed and folded.

Now that spring has come to the hollow, everywhere I look I see babies. Up on the Jaffee Farm, not only are there the young piglets, but a new brood of peeping chicks. The yellow little balls of feathers are so damn cute. I want about 500 of them for my yard. I don't think the deer would be terribly happy about that, but I imagine the coyotes would have one hell of a party.

Speaking of deer, each day I look into the forest with anticipation because I know it's time for the first fawns of the season to make an appearance. When they show up, I don't even pretend to be calm. I let out a whoop and call everyone I know to let them know the fawns have made their debut. My favorite deer take a good deal of pride in bringing their new additions and showing them off. I do sense some competition between the mothers.

This weekend is the huge Tractor Parade down the river in Callicoon. This grand procession of tractors from over the decades causes the streets to be packed with appreciative crowds. Prizes are given and this year Turkey Hollow is rooting for our neighbor, John Forquhar. His beautifully restored 1939 Farmall Tractor is a sure bet to grab some attention and, hopefully, some blue ribbons. John is working on a 1932 version in his barn out back and we can't wait until he cleans up on the awards with that one. For a good time, you just can't beat dozens of tractors driving back and forth on Main Street in Callicoon.

Next week will find us all sitting on the edge of our chairs for the return of "The Great Trout" in the Livingston Manor Trout Parade, one of the biggest celebrations of the year. "The Great Trout" is not akin to the "The Great Pumpkin" of Charles Schultz's *Peanuts* comic strip but is still cause for great excitement. The parade marks the first time we can actually see water in our rivers since the winter ice melted. My understanding is that it will be one of the biggest parades ever to honor The Great Trout.

Only seven more days to go.

Moments of Pride

As Gay Pride rolls around this year, I remember my first Pride Parade, which was about almost forty years ago in Hollywood. I wasn't yet out so was afraid to watch from the sidewalk of Hollywood Boulevard, fearing that if anyone saw me just watching they would know that I was gay. Two years later, as an openly gay man, I found myself walking in the parade with about 15,000 people, in total awe of how many had joined together to express our pride. Times sure have changed since.

This Gay Pride got me thinking of all those special moments over the last four decades where events gave me an overwhelming sense of pride. Those times when tears came to my eyes, knowing what an honor it was to be part of such a powerful, kind and just LGBT community.

Never have I felt more pride than the day I decided to come

out of the closet. I was enveloped both in total fear and total exhilaration. Never again would I have to hide, lie about myself or be alone. It was the beginning of my life as a free man.

The first black tie dinner held by the Municipal Elections Committee of Los Angeles (MELCA) was another milestone. This first political PAC in the history of the community went to the Beverly Wilshire Ballroom and over $40,000 was raised in one night. Only the City Attorney of Los Angeles, Bert Pines, and City Councilwomen Peggy Stevenson had the courage to attend that dinner. All of us who organized the gala stared at each other in disbelief that we had succeeded in pulling off such a magnificent event.

How can I forget the night we defeated Proposition 6 in California? We had been behind three to one in this initiative that would have banned homosexual schoolteachers from working in classrooms. Thousands of us were jammed into the ballroom of the Beverly Hilton Hotel and thousands more had to be turned away by the fire marshal as the returns showed we were going to win. I will forever recall the moment I had the honor of announcing that we had won. We cheered, hugged everyone in sight and cried tears of joy.

The entire HIV/AIDS epidemic, especially in the 1980s, was a time of darkness but also of great pride. Never has a community been tested more and not only survived but passed with flying colors. We protested, went to jail, took care of our sick and dying, reformed the FDA, created healthcare institutions, fought against discrimination, and stood proudly and defiantly against those who wanted us to become victims. In the blackness of a pandemic, we found our collective political clout and strength.

In 1991, Governor Peter Wilson vetoed AB 101, which was a bill that would have outlawed LGBT discrimination in California. There's no way to describe my pride as thousands and thousands of LGBT citizens poured into the streets of Los Angeles night after night, blocking traffic and refusing to sit quietly.

One of the more historic moments came in May 1992 when President Clinton gave his famous "I Have a Vision and You Are Part of It" speech. People crammed into the Hollywood Palace wondering if Clinton really would take a tough public stand on LGBT rights in front of the press. Riding with Clinton that night to the event, he said to me, "I am leaving a staff that doesn't want me to give this speech to a place where no one believes I am going to give it." Without hesitation, he outlined a world where LGBT people would be free if he were elected.

This was followed up with that year's Democratic National Convention where the openly gay Roberta Achtenberg and Bob Hattoy spoke from the stage in prime time, while all over the floor of the Convention there were signs that read "LGBT Voters for Clinton." In his acceptance speech, Clinton used the word "gay," which at that time was a huge victory, and the Convention hall, straight and gay, went nuts.

Then there was the fateful day when twenty of us got arrested at the White House protesting DADT with very little support from the community and a hostile and swift reaction from the White House.

The 1993 March on Washington was one more incredibly proud moment with over 600,000 LGBT people and their allies in attendance. Not only were we as a community emerging from the darkness of the AIDS epidemic but also experiencing newly found political power. There were people as far as the eye could see.

I am so proud and honored to call this community my own.

Bad News and Good News

The first hints of trouble started late Tuesday afternoon. It was unbearably hot and humid which is very unusual for the hills. The clouds were building and there wasn't a breeze. As I sat on my back porch rocking, it was getting really dark directly west of me.

Cats Hollow is a little over five miles, as the crow flies, from my house. It lies just west over my mountain peak, down the neighboring valley and up the next hollow. Like Turkey Hollow, it is home to people who love the Catskills and find living in them a gift. As a neighbor dropped by for a quick visit, we both remarked how the clouds weren't moving at all.

The weather service had issued a warning that these hollows could expect some rough thunderstorms, but that was just the weather we get up here.

Around 7:30 P.M. on Tuesday night, the thunder and lightning began over toward Cats Hollow. It was an unbelievable show from my porch, and I don't ever recall seeing so much lightning. Usually when it starts raining in the next valley I get it rather quickly, but it took over an hour to move five miles to reach Turkey Hollow. When it hit, it hit hard. The rain came down in sheets with over three to four inches in the two hours that it took the storm to pass. Never in my life had I experienced so much lightning. It was like an aerial bombardment in a war with strikes hitting every thirty seconds somewhere close. Water poured everywhere.

Now I have to admit folks, I love rough weather and pride myself on being entertained by it. This time I was scared—just plain and simple scared. There wasn't anything normal about it. The storm was mean and violent. I couldn't see the back of my hand. My cats had hid under the bed, and I was quickly bemoaning the fact that I couldn't fit under there with them. It was wicked, raw, nasty nature at its worst.

As night fell, I wondered how my neighbors had fared. There was no water in my basement, no trees down and no fire from lightning that I could see anywhere. I had a good feeling as I went to sleep.

The next morning brought the bad news from Cats Hollow. The storm had indeed stalled just five miles from me and dropped over eight inches of rain. A massive wall of water had swept through the Hollow, taking everything in its path. At least four people were missing and maybe as many as seven might be gone. Everyone was in shock.

As soon as it was safe and the bridges were checked, I headed into town to get information. We still get information up here the

old fashioned way, either at Peck's Store or Johnny's Barbershop.
You can find out anything at Johnny's, which still has the old-
fashioned barber pole outside, two chairs inside, lots of hunting
magazines and good community gossip. We men, however, like to
think we don't gossip. We just swap information at Johnny's that
will make the community a better place.

As expected, everything that needed to be known had reached
Johnny's. The town was filled with rescue trucks, FEMA vans and
State Troopers heading to Roscoe to set up a staging area for Cats
Hollow. People in this neck of the woods are used to floods and
Livingston Manor was badly flooded just a year ago this week. As
Johnny says, "It is just part of the price we pay in these hills to live
in God's nature."

Being used to floods didn't mean they didn't care, and as I
have seen over and over since I moved to Turkey Hollow, caring
is alive and well in the Catskills. People immediately knew their
roles and got busy. Food was prepared by everyone for the rescue
workers. Volunteer fire departments for miles were involved in
search and rescue. Others gathered clothing and food for the
families affected. Sadness was a way of life that day as word came
on who had lost loved ones.

Bad news in Turkey Hollow this week, but I was reminded
again how powerful the concept of neighbors is to Americans and
how we look after each other in tough times, even though often
our government fails to do so.

The next day amid the devastation, life came back in full force
to Turkey Hollow in the form of twin fawns. It turns out that
Kate and Attila the deer had twins instead of just the one. Two
little fawns, Bambi and Dancer, played in my backyard most of

the morning as Kate looked on. I laughed, took pictures and was riveted with their antics. With the fawns' tiny white spots, cute small faces and fragile legs, who couldn't help but to fall in love with them?

They reminded me that even in the darkest moments in a community there is beauty. There is always hope for tomorrow. This time that hope came in two little fawns named Bambi and Dancer.

The County Fair

One of the great disappointments in moving to Turkey Hollow is that there really isn't an old-fashioned county fair here. Totally expected to be able to relive childhood moments, eating cotton candy, corn dogs and homemade pies. Even believed that at my age I could go to the carnival and brave the amusement rides that we rode again and again as kids. Of course, which one of our friends brought home blue ribbons and which of the local girls would become Miss Cumberland County Fair was on everyone's mind back then.

The Cumberland County Fair was a big deal. It covered acres and acres, and no one in the surrounding farming areas would dream of missing it. People came from three counties and prepared for it all summer long. Those special secret recipes would be snuck out of hiding to compete in the pie and cake contests. Winning first place for a pie would not only bring a blue ribbon but also bragging rights to the winner, who usually strutted her victory with outlandish pride. The losers would gather in the corner of the fair tent and gossip about how ungracious the winner was acting and maybe that she even bent the rules to win. It was a hard loss for many to swallow.

Not sure if this is true, but it seemed as though no one else won first place as long as Mrs. Woodruff entered her pies. If you have never had a slice of her glorious confections then you really haven't eaten pie. Don't know what the elderly grande dame of pies did, but one bite sent you on an unbelievable trip of pleasure. Today, I have suspicions that very proper lady secretly snuck hallucinating mushrooms into her dessert and made us lose control. Despite the sore losers, we all would line up to taste her winning entry, and she would brush away comments by demurely responding, "Oh, thank you, but it was nothing. I just whipped something up quickly in the kitchen to make the County Fair on time." Of course, that comment would send the losers into fits of rage.

Continuing on a high from the sugary pie, I would head over to the area housing all the animals. Tents would be filled with cows, pigs, horses, sheep and dogs all competing for that ribbon. Many of the fine animals were raised as 4-H projects by young kids. They spent days preparing their animals for the judging. A blue ribbon often meant a fair bit of money for the winner and often a death sentence for the animal. Never could quite get my head around how you could build that special relationship with the animal that rewards you with nobility by winning and then go and send it off to slaughter. Where was PETA when we needed them? But I loved at a young age touching and petting the cream of the crop of our surrounding area's animals. Even the pigs were at their best, cleaned from the mud, a "pretty in pink" look, and snorting for attention.

Heading to the rides and stopping for that cotton candy and corn dog, we had to pass the sideshow. For years I was not allowed to go inside to see what seemed to be the great wonders for the world brought directly to us: "The Bearded Lady," "The Shortest Person in the World," and "The Man Who Eats Fire." Several of us kids attempted to sneak into the back of the sideshow but got caught before we could even catch a glimpse of these amazing individuals. My father would go in, and eagerly I would await his exit to question him endlessly about what was inside that mysterious tent of the world's greatest. He would only laugh and say it was too "scary" to tell me, which made it even more desirable.

No fair would be complete without winning a stuffed animal, a cupie doll or some silly prize in the game tents. No Pacman game in these tents. You had to throw a ball, shoot a rifle or toss the rings just right to win the coveted prizes. My parents would swear the games were rigged, but how come I always won a prize after spending tens of dollars to win something worth about two dollars? Rigged? I don't think so. I won on pure unadulterated skill.

As we ended our visit to the fair, we were exhausted and filled with junk food. The walk to the car seemed like an endless journey when it seemed so close in the morning. Falling asleep in the backseat of our old 1946 DeSoto, I would dream of seeing the Bearded Lady, and she looked simply beautiful in her mystery.

Homecoming

A brand new bear arrived two days ago. The heavy black bear appears to be only about a year old and just getting the lay of the land. Hearing my cats go crazy sitting on the windowsill in my house was my first tip off of the new visitor. Looking outside to see why they were so agitated, I spotted him—loving the back yard, stretching out, wandering around and seeking treats hidden among the wildflowers. He posed for a few shots taken through my window, but when I entered the back porch he bolted like lightning into woods. Had no idea they could travel so fast and it was an important reminder as I watched him jump over logs and bushes like a white tale deer.

Note to David: Don't attempt to out run a bear—not going to happen.

Determined not to be overshadowed by some stupid,

lumbering bear, a young fawn finally started hanging out in the yard and not running every time there was the slightest noise. There have been very few fawns this year compared to the last couple of years. The locals think it is the brutally cold and snowy winter we had. Does will abort their babies depending on the supply of food. They can abort one at a time depending on how tough the winter is. Usually I have had five or six fawns dancing around by this time, but right now I have had only one little beauty take up housekeeping with his mother.

On the front porch I have either a bird condo or a bird that is a total slut. It is not clear to me which. The nest was built quickly after the front porch was completed and has been in use since I moved in over three years ago. We currently are on our second set of babies this year. The first was a group of four crowding in the nest. Now we have two babies just born. Could be two mothers or the same mother who happens to be a sex addict. Let's see if they go for a third time before winter hits again.

In addition, the old regulars have shown up for their summer vacations. "Hooter the Owl" has taken up his stand on the tree with the huge limbs in the backyard. He is the biggest damn owl I have ever seen. Silently he sits blending into the foliage waiting for a very foolish mouse to make an attempt to dash across the backyard to seek sanctuary in my home. The mouse rarely completes his journey, but if he does outsmart Hooter the Owl, he is summarily greeted by Uganda who is a mouser extraordinaire. The poor mice in Turkey Hollow lead a very precarious life.

The two massive hawks also have taken residence, returning from their winter home in Latin America. Not sure if they are Spanish or English-speaking hawks but they're beautiful. Someone said it was rare to see these particular hawks in these parts—and they sure act as if they are special, constantly flying over the backyard in apparent blatant reconnaissance missions. There is no question that the are violating the air space agreements of Turkey Hollow in search of a little helpless bird to eat.

Even more migrants have shown up in the last couple of weeks, and it appears that everyone has arrived home for the summer. The newcomers are looking a little out of place, but the animal kingdom in the Hollow is doing its best to welcome them—either as friends or as dinner.

Flowers

My back acreage is filled with thousands of yellow Black-eyed Susans. The view from the porch is like a carpet of yellow for deer and fawns to play and lie upon. Earlier, it had been a sea of some sort of white flower, and we all are wondering here in Turkey Hollow if there is a "third act" to follow the yellow. Maybe some sort of red? Flowers have always had a special place in my life mostly because of my Grandpa Grove.

Never minding that we were surrounded by fields containing crops of tomatoes, asparagus, corn, peas, potatoes and beets, Grandpa had to plant a garden. So what did he plant? Tomatoes, asparagus, corn, peas, potatoes and beets. He added a strawberry patch and a pumpkin patch for variety, and it all took a great deal of effort to keep it in good shape all summer.

But to me, what made the garden worthwhile was that he also

grew row after row of beautiful flowers, from gladiolas to zinnias to marigolds. The rainbow of colors was so vivid and beautiful. We would walk into the garden each day and cut flowers for the house and even neighbors would stop by in their pickup trucks to admire his beauties. Hard, red-faced farmers in their dusty bib overalls would suddenly become flower children as Grandpa Grove offered them fresh-cut flowers to take home to their wives. Aunt Millie's vegetable stand along Route 40 sold them to the rich folks from Philly passing by on their way to the Jersey beaches. The garden became a place of pride for the entire family.

When I think of flowers in childhood for some reason I always think of funerals. Dying meant two things back home: incredible food and beautiful flowers. The neighbors would fill table after table with their best dishes, cakes and pies—enough to feed the Russian Army. The wake (or "viewing," as we used to call it) was the first time we would see the flowers that people sent in memory of the deceased. After viewing the newly departed and remarking what a good job the funeral director had done with making up the body, there was not a whole lot to do except every once in a while prying some hysterical person from the casket. So to pass time, we would look at the huge baskets of flowers and see who sent them. With biting wit and maybe a tinge of bitchiness, we would comment on each bouquet and judge if the mourner had spent enough. Some were so tasteless in their intent that it would send tongues wagging. A farmer's wife spying a spray from the deceased mistress would give a shocked look, sniff in the air, and loudly proclaim that the flowers should have been red to match the harlot's values.

In the sixties, during the anti-Vietnam War protests, flowers became a weapon for the peace movement. As national guard troops were called out to quell campus unrest or the federal troops sent into Chicago in 1968 for the Democratic Convention, the flower children would go down the line of guns with bayonets and gently place a single flower in the barrel of each gun. We placed them in our hair and predictably sang the anti-war song "Where Have All the Flowers Gone?"

And now all these years later, as the sun slips below the horizon here in Turkey Hollow, the wild flowers are so life affirming and just simply beautiful: another quiet dusk with birds chirping, frogs crocking and deer snorting. The fawns bounce around in the flowers and seem to get a high off them. Their parents lay in them and bemused, watch over their gamboling youngsters.

Meet George and Daniel

Sometimes I think we all feel being gay started in San Francisco in the 1950s. Even so, I have often wondered what it must have been like during pioneer days when groups of men would travel together for months, on cattle drives, on great adventures. Or what it was like in small frontier towns where everyone knew everyone else's personal business. Well, my sister Patsy, helped answer that question.

In her research she discovered a book called *The Annals of Buffalo Valley (1755-1855)*, which was released in 1877. In the book, which takes place in central Pennsylvania, there is a wonderful entry in 1810. If these guys aren't gay, then no one is gay. I loved the description of the two moving in together and arguing over the housekeeper. I hope you enjoy this as much as I did.

Buffalo Valley, 1810

Daniel Doudle was an acquaintance of Governor Snyder in his boyhood, and in more mature years he would sometimes pay the Governor a visit, at Selinsgrove, and thus formed acquaintance with George Kremer. After George moved to Derrstown, and established himself in business and a bachelor's hall there, Daniel extended his visits thither, and become so much pleased that he resolved to forsake York altogether, and remain with George. Accordingly, he sent for his money, a considerable stock of dollars, and took up his abode in Derrstown. He and George agreed very well, for George humored him all his whims, but he quarreled sadly with old Peggy Miller, the housekeeper. Sometimes he would come in a towering passion to George, with "Now, George, I can't live with the old devil any longer. Just send me off to Selinsgrove, to Simon, and he will send me to York." "Well, well" said George, "Roan (Clark) or John shall take you and your money in the cart to Selinsgrove as soon you like." "Do you think," Daniel would reply, "I would trust myself with the damned rascals? They would murder me for my money before we got half way to Selinsgrove." Then an argument would commence on the honesty of Roan and John, which generally lasted until Daniel, in his rage against these two, had forgotten his wrath toward old Peggy. At length, Daniel fell into the hands of an old Methodist woman, who, by her exhortations, made considerable impression on him. After spending an evening at Mother Grove's, Daniel came home with a face so solemn and important that the whole family noticed it, and knowing where he had been the clerk followed him on his retreat to bed, and peeped and listened at his door. Daniel locked his door, looked carefully around, undressed (taking off his hat the last of all, as was his usual custom), kneeled by the bedside, and commenced thus: "O, Lord God," then ensued a long pause. Up rose Daniel, exclaiming, "It is too damned cold to pray here!" and jumped into bed. Whether Daniel made another effort to pray is uncertain. He once acted godfather for one of his friend's children. The clergyman asked the name of the child. Daniel, understanding him to ask his name, promptly replied: "Daniel Doudle, to be sure. Don't you know me any more?" Daniel, at this time eighty years of age, usually dressed himself once a day in state, in a blue silk-velvet coat, white vest, ruffled shirt, brown silk-velvet small-clothes, and turned up shoes, and paraded himself down to the river bank and back, to exhibit himself to the ladies. He lived to be one hundred and one or one hundred and two years of age, dying in August 1828, at Mr. Kremer's, near Middleburg, where his bones rest with those of his friends, Frederick Evans and George Kremer. Certainly three more singular men were never so intimately associated in life and rest so close together in the solemn silence of death.

The Sanctuary of Summer

When I was in grade school, the summer days lasted forever. The hours seemed to pass so much slower and there was time for everything before collapsing in bed at night.

Growing up in the country, I would wake to the smell of freshly plowed fields and the sounds of a crop duster making a final pass over the land. At sunrise, I could hear a chorus of birds in the pine trees outside my window arguing about who would do what task for the day. Awakening with a wonderful lazy summer feeling, I would snuggle deeper into sun-dried sheets, hoping that Mom or Dad wouldn't find me under the covers. Some days, when the morning dawn was perfectly still, I would know that it was going to be a scorcher. I'd just slip on a pair of shorts and live in them.

Summer was wonderful. It was a break from the rest of the year. There were no blizzards to struggle with and no homework or report cards. I had to help around the farm, but the work was outdoors and always promised some sort of exciting adventure. For some reason, all the problems of the world seemed to hold off until fall.

The summer months are the setting for some of my fondest childhood memories—trips to the ocean, big games of hide and seek with the adults on a Sunday afternoon, swimming naked in the irrigation ponds with my buddies, catching tadpoles, chasing lightning bugs to put in jars and listening to the adults at twilight as they rocked on the porch telling stories that riveted our attention.

During the season, I learned to be alone with nature. Even as a young child, it was considered safe for me to take walks deep into the woods and play in the streams. Climbing the trees to look over the fields of crops, I could see forever. I would spend the day exploring on my own, building forts in the deep dense forest to protect myself from outside intruders…especially adults. Sleeping along a stream in the warm sunlight, I would succumb to an afternoon nap.

Summer is still special for me.

The mountaintop and the valley come alive with the colors of wildflowers, green firs and a dense forest filled with hidden wildlife. The mornings are still announced by the squabbling birds. The wind teases the thick, green leaves in my woods, creating a gentle music that I'll long for in the darkness of winter. With long sunlit days, there is simply more time to relax in my rocking chair on the screened porch and take in the beauty of the Hollow.

For the wildlife, it is the best of times.

There are no hunters looking for trophies to place on their walls. Attila, with his six-point rack, can walk around free and unworried of humans chasing him simply because of his majestic appearance. Little fawns dance all over the yard, chasing each other and annoying their ever-protective mothers. With a slight kick of the back leg, the does teach the young fawns to eat on their own and that their free meal days are over.

Even the deer seem more relaxed, lounging in the backyard to take in the sun.

At night as I sit on my porch sharing stories of great past adventures with young friends, the yard is filled with hundreds of lightning bugs creating a backdrop right out of *Midsummer's Night Dream*. The sounds of coyotes intermingle with owls, creating a summer night chorus to enchant even the most cynical among us. City folk visiting for the night and more used to the sounds of fire engines than wildlife, jump as they hear something walking in the moonlit night. They, too, feel a sense of adventure in the Hollow.

During August, it's oddly permissible to tune out the sounds of campaigning politicians. You are allowed to enjoy coffee in peace on the porch in the morning without having to read about world's troubles. You can reminisce about more innocent times from youth. And you can enjoy the lazy season's sweet air and warm sun without guilt.

Summer has always been a sanctuary. Now up here in Turkey Hollow, it still is for Attila, Kate and me.

Quiet and Lonely in the Hills

This week, I was thrilled by the response to the *New York Times* article on my life here in Turkey Hollow. Countless readers, friends and long lost contacts emailed and called to catch up and learn more about my rural sanctuary in upstate New York. Inevitably, however, almost all of them asked the same sensitive question: "Aren't you lonely up there?"

This question is not new to me. Since I moved here, many of my friends and especially my political allies have inquired endlessly about my loneliness and isolation. I usually brush their questions off with some quick, witty one-liner before assuring them that I am doing just fine and moving the conversation along to other topics. I've come to realize, however, that treating such a loving inquiry in this way is just not consistent with the honest and simple life I have built in Turkey Hollow.

The article actually gave me a gift for which I am very grateful. With so many people inquiring about my existence in Turkey Hollow, I had to confront the question myself. Offering one-liners to deflect the issue and then getting busy feeding apples to the deer isn't an honest way to process the choices that I have made. Reflecting on my own loneliness hasn't been easy, but the process of finding personal enlightenment has been exhilarating.

You see, I live in Turkey Hollow because of the HIV/AIDS epidemic. Those of us who have survived the last twenty-five years have chosen many different ways to get on with life. At times, I have blissfully continued on as though the sickness, death, and abandonment by many of our institutions and certainly our government had never happened. Those painful early years, when so much was lost, are just too horrible to relive, to confront and even to understand. It is difficult to process that my community lived through such horror, let alone me personally.

These memories are recalled more easily, however, within the context of the LGBT community's heroic struggle against HIV/AIDS. Together, we somehow found solutions to insurmountable problems, saving those we could and celebrating those we could not. We found the gifts in our darkness and are still offering them to the world. Instead of fear and panic, we embraced our struggle and built upon it. After all, isn't courage just a lack of options?

Nevertheless, the trauma of that time remains, even here in my new home. Sometimes I am lonely living in Turkey Hollow, but I have been lonely in some form since the beginning of the HIV/AIDS epidemic.

How could I not be lonely? I lost hundreds of friends to AIDS.

Within a two-year period, I gave more than ninety eulogies for friends who had died of AIDS, most of whom were under forty years of age. One activist group that I belonged to in the late-1970s had thirty male members, and I'm the only one who's still alive. I spent most of my thirties and forties taking care of the sick and dying, fighting for our survival, and struggling to hold on to some kind of equilibrium, so I wouldn't become bitter at my own country for letting its young die without a fight.

Yes, we were courageous and noble and powerful and beautiful through it all, but no matter how you cut it, to live through that period was simply a horror. All of us who made it through were wounded in some way, and all of us have had to come to terms with what we experienced.

For me, I have had to grow old without my peers. Without my friends to share the history of those joyous moments before AIDS hit—the flourishing of the Castro Street area, the excitement of the sexual revolution, the sheer high of coming out of the closet and the early days of our struggle for freedom. What a time it was to be alive and to be gay. I loved every day before the darkness hit. I would love to be able to sit around at dinner parties with friends no longer here and reminisce of those glorious days.

As I emerged from that profound experience, I made some powerful commitments to myself. One, that I would never let those who've died be forgotten. Two, I would live life as if I was living for us all. Three, I would refuse to become a victim and an object of pity. Four, I would take the gifts we received from their lives and offer them to the world. Finally, I would surround myself with beauty, joy, nature, loving people and be grateful for each day.

In Turkey Hollow, my loneliness is surrounded by beauty. When guests come, I have intense, wonderful visits with them instead of quick, short dinners. My mind has never been more creative and excited. The horrors of those years seem so far away from me now. The fawns remind me of renewal, the seasons of change and the quiet of peace.

Yes, I am lonely at times. Given my life's journey, there is no place, no matter how crowded, where I can't be lonely. But I am happy here, surrounded by beauty, energized by extraordinary visits with my dear friends, living at one with nature and feeling more productive and at peace than ever.

Heat Wave

God, it's getting even hotter up here. Sure, compared to the drenching, sweltering heat that New York or Washington, D.C. are experiencing, the Hollow is just a cool breeze. However, I have gotten used to the cool of the mountains and the nearby rivers, so it seems very hot indeed. When it edges into the upper-eighties here we start complaining in Johnny's Barbershop how hot it has become. The old-timers get out their fans and the porches become the centers of all social interaction. Cold lemonade and iced tea are readily available in most homes, and the kids make Kool-Aid ice cubes. The cats and dogs stretch way out on the cool textures of the floor, and it is almost impossible to move them until they hear the can opener signaling dinner. Then they jump quickly up, and they start rubbing against your leg as if they have been your best friend all day.

Driving back to the Hollow from town, I passed kids swimming in the river, and it took me back to my youth on the farm.

Long heat waves are not good for farmers and my Dad used to dread them. They dry out the crops and instill fears of a possible crippling drought. Back then we had no satellites giving us long range weather forecasts, and the farmers were left to their own instincts. If the heat lasted more than a week and there were no gathering storm clouds, you could see the worry on the adult faces.

For us kids, heat meant hardly any clothes, skinny dipping in the irrigation pond down in the field or creating our own "pools" made out of any materials we could find. We would take our long wooden picnic benches and create a square with them. Then we would take one of the canvas tops from the steel body trucks and spread it over the four benches. Suddenly we would have our own "swimming pool" that was about three feet deep to splash around and soak the heat out of our bodies. Of course, if we would play too hard we would knock over one of the benches and there would go our pool.

At night, a hot summer evening meant gathering on the front porch of the house. Everyone sat on it, dinner was had on it, and we would sleep on it at night. It quite simply became the center of our home. Before nightfall, it would be my job to hose down the porch to get the day's heat out of it. Grandpa Grove would rock away and share stories. Dad would take a break from the fields and join us for dinner. Mom would make a cool meal of sliced fresh Jersey tomatoes, potato salad, hot dogs and rolls and frosty iced tea. The fireflies would light up the outstretched flat fields.

If we were lucky and Dad didn't have to harvest peas at night, we would drive to the local drive-in for frozen custard. One time in the early 1950s we all went to see the original *King Kong* with Fay Wray. For weeks after seeing the movie, I would be asleep on the front porch or my small bedroom with the windows wide open and wake up in the middle of the night screaming that King Kong was on the roof. It drove my parents nuts, but I still believe today that he was on the roof and I saved the family by alerting them.

So tonight, unlike my grandfather, I will leave on the central air up here in Turkey Hollow. However, I will go out on the porch and take my place in the big rocker. The more things change, the more they stay the same.

Childhood Dreams

The other day, one of my best friends said to me, "Mixner you are really lucky. Most all of your dreams have come true."

Of course, when someone makes a statement like that your first reaction is to protest loudly. One, because such a statement implies that you are finished with life and two, because one feels slightly guilty to have been allowed to experience so much in one lifetime. Not to protest would look like I wasn't humble. Trust me, I am humbled and have been humbled over and over. My friend was right. Most of my childhood dreams have come true in some form.

Now don't get me wrong. My life has been turbulent and at times it has been shattered. Great wealth has never come to me. I lived through the peak of the AIDS epidemic and gave an endless number of eulogies. I have often seen and experienced the sordid and painful side of life.

But all of that is overshadowed by the fact that through it all, I have realized most of my life dreams.

As a child, I was enchanted with the world outside my rural and isolated existence. *Life* magazine was my vehicle to visit far away places and famous people. I used to wait by the mailbox for its arrival every Friday, when Mr. Schaffer would drive up our narrow road in his old 1930's Dodge. What an inspiration those pages were for me.

I would run back into the house and lie on the living room floor, savoring each page in the warm afternoon sunlight. I wanted to see and experience the places photographed in the magazine. I wanted to meet the leaders that the reporters interviewed. The wonders of the world were waiting for me, and I was filled with restlessness until I could venture out into the world.

My most cherished dream has evolved during six decades of life. At first I just wanted to witness the history of my times, to be a bystander and see first hand what all that was in *Life* magazine. As my life progressed, I realized that I was indeed witnessing history and that was not enough. I wanted to meet the leaders that were making that history and to touch them, to say hello and maybe even engage one or two in conversation. Eventually, in the most modest of ways, I have been allowed to participate in making history through the great civil rights movements of our times.

My childhood dreams also included a list of places in the world that I wanted to see before I died. I started that list when I was just ten years old, and I finally finished it with a visit to the Great Wall of China. Some of the other places on that list were the Nile River, Africa and its wonderful wildlife, the beautiful city of St.

Petersburg, Christmas in Paris, and a houseboat in Amsterdam. I was filled with total joy as I experienced each new culture and sight. And as I stood on the Great Wall, I was overwhelmed with a sense of completion and accomplishment.

My friend's comment made me pause and think: *Was there anything that I had dreamed that had not come true?* My first reaction was that I never got that ranch that I had so dreamed about—a safe haven for endangered animals. I even had a location picked out in Montana and plans for a stunning ranch house with equally stunning ranch hands.

But then suddenly, I realized I am living that dream now on a smaller scale. I have six acres of wonderful land on the top of a mountain that has deer, bobcats, coyotes, wild turkeys, bear and other creatures. In fact, my little ranch is filled with wildlife and it is beautiful land.

Now, I believe one should never stop dreaming. I still buy Lotto tickets every week. No, I really don't think I will win but I love dreaming about how I would use the money to help others and, of course, for myself. I have a new list of things to do and to accomplish.

Dreams, after all, to paraphrase Keats, are not a time and place but they are in your heart and a state of mind.

Princess Diana Remembered

Today is the anniversary of the death of Princess Diana. Dozens of media specials, books and articles have overwhelmed us over the last few weeks about this tragic young princess. They have gone into every aspect of her life claiming mental instability, too many affairs and consistent bad judgment. All claim to be based on fact. Who knows what is truth and what is fiction, made up solely to make a profit? I personally have no idea, nor do I expect that we will ever be able to sort through the salacious rumors to find the truth.

This much I do know. She was a beautiful woman, though flawed, frightened and full of youthful naiveté as she was thrown into the royal family. She served her people well and died a very tragic death before her time.

In the 1980s, when the entire world seemed unable to even

touch a person with HIV/AIDS, she went to a London hospital, walked in, and shook hands with a person with AIDS who was in a wheelchair. At the time, it was a very important moment of recognition for those of us fighting the epidemic every day, seemingly on our own. We can't possibly forget her courage or grace.

Her love for children who were ill, in need or maimed was unmatched. She held the AIDS orphan of Uganda in her lap, the sick children of England in her arms and the children maimed from land mines received her hugs. No child was too poor, too sick or too battered for her. They were all her children.

At great risk to herself, Princess Diana was determined to make the world deal with land mines when most world leaders ignored the issue. Who can forget when she traveled to Angola and literally walked through a dangerous mine field to make sure the world got the message? She made sure we knew that dozens of people, mostly children, were being killed each day. And she told the world that it cost just $3 to make a land mine, while it took many thousands to remove them.

While she was the charismatic glamorous international media star, she was truly the "People's Princess." She seemed at home with working class stiffs, the poor and the needy. There was an endless supply of compassion and love that she dispensed to all who would receive it. When she walked and held the hand of the man in the wheelchair with AIDS, she forever became my princess.

My Youthful Innocence

Up here in Turkey Hollow it really doesn't make sense to put out a yard sign loudly proclaiming your choice for a candidate for public office. No one goes down this one lane dirt road except my wise neighbor Wayne Keller. Now, Old Man Keller is an old-fashioned conscientious citizen who holds this country dear to his heart. His passion this year is the immigration issue and he is articulate and powerful on it. He doesn't need me to tell him how to vote; indeed, he would no doubt chide me for littering the beautiful countryside with a silly political sign.

However, I do miss the days in my youth when I would cover myself with buttons, wear silly hats, put out lawn signs, have the mandatory bumper sticker affixed to the car, and leave college to work on different issues or campaigns. Maybe it is the reason why I never finished my university education. Self-righteousness was my sword and pity the poor person who disagreed with me. There were no shades of gray for me. People were either good or evil. Issues were perfectly clear and there were no complexities to them.

My politics were shaped by movements and a few heroic candidates. I was trained and informed and inspired by the civil rights movement; I learned leadership in the anti-Vietnam War movement, I found my courage in the LGBT movement.

President Kennedy was my first "candidate crush." Being fourteen, his speeches and words inspired me into a lifetime of politics. He convinced me of not only my moral obligation to serve those in need but that the world was actually waiting for me to do it. You would have to count me as one of the classic "Kennedy's Children": young people he inspired into public service. The youth of America would wait for hours to catch a glimpse of him, so riveted were we by his special grace and his moving speeches. Quotes from his speeches were repeated to each other. We were filled with youthful innocence and we so believed we could change the world.

The day he was inaugurated on a snowy, bitterly cold Washington, D.C. morning, almost every television set in America was turned on to the ceremony. On our living room floor, I laid in front of our very small Philco television screen and listened to his call to go into the world. In his speech, a simple phrase became a way of life for Americans: "Ask not what your country can do for you but what you can do for your country." Thousands answered his call and joined the Peace Corps and VISTA. We cared about the poor and wanted to end segregation. We headed south at a very young age to end decades of discrimination. We demanded free speech in our universities and respect for different ideas and diversity of people.

We believed in his words and he believed in us.

The day he was assassinated I lost my youthful innocence. From then on, there were less buttons and more doubt. The world indeed could be a very dark and complex place. Fewer quick answers were on the tip of my tongue. Instead of buttons, I wore black that horrible November weekend. And carried that grief into my politics for years to come. Black and white dissolved into a muddle of gray.

As a young person of the sixties, we saw Bobby Kennedy shot, Martin Luther King shot, the four little girls blown up in Birmingham, the police dogs attacking peaceful demonstrators, and our teenage buddies coming back in boxes from Vietnam. Dying for justice, filling the jails and fleeing the country to protest the War were simply parts of our lives. We were toughened quickly. Many in pain withdrew from the battles, unable to deal with the ugliness of the world. Yet somehow, deep inside of me, there was a strong determination never to give up what John Kennedy gave me—which was a profound belief that I could create change.

What an amazing gift to give to the young. I will forever be grateful.

Fall

❧

Back to School

The signs of fall are currently all over Turkey Hollow. The leaves are rapidly changing, some having even already fallen from what were until recently, thick, green trees of summer. I'm not quite sure how bright the colors will be this year and can't remember if it is a good year for leaves if it has been a dry summer or if it is a wet summer. Expecting our first frost/freeze as soon as tomorrow evening, the windows in the bedroom are now only half open, the comforter has been brought out of storage and the cats are snuggling deep into it at night.

Local kids going back to school is one of the surer autumnal signs. Some county students started even before Labor Day and the others right after it. That all seems so early for me.

When I grew up back on our New Jersey farm, schools would never open until the summer crops were done and that usually meant the third week of September. And they would never stay open after Memorial Day. Every able body was needed to plow, pick, and move irrigation pipe. My elementary school was a very small building in Daretown with wooden floors and big windows overlooking the fields. Clearly, years before, some farmer had given the land and our small school was cut into the fields. The first four grades were on one side and an auditorium separated the top four grades on the other side. Outside there was a volunteer-made baseball diamond and one set of swings and even a jungle gym.

Early on in my schooling, there was no place to eat the lunch you brought every day in a brown bag. Noting the problem, the farm families got together and hand-built wooden benches and wooden tables for the basement. Turkey dinners and cake sales were employed to offset the costs of the kitchen equipment. Upon its completion, we all then were guaranteed at least one hot meal each day. Huge cans of stewed tomatoes were sent by the State and I hated them. But there was a real sense of pride that we all got together and created this very rough cafeteria in the basement of the school.

Most all of our teachers were farmer's wives who had gotten a "teacher's certificate" from nearby Glassboro State College. Not much was required to obtain that certificate and as a result, many of us left the school further behind in academics than the other students at regional Woodstown High School. Old books, poorly prepared teachers, no music, no art and other subpar essentials pretty much guaranteed a subpar education. Still, we said the Lord's Prayer every morning, consistently pledged allegiance to the flag, celebrated Christmas and had two days off for Easter, despite the presence of some Jewish students. I always felt bad for them.

Getting to the schoolhouse itself was quite the adventure. We had to rise at six A.M. in order to eat breakfast and get ready for school. We would sit in the window of the farmhouse and watch for the bus driven by Mr. Egan coming over the hill by the Garrison farm. Then we would grab our coats and books and rush outside, down to the rural road for him to stop and pick us up. The high school students always got to sit in the front of the bus and those picked up earlier would save seats for their friends. We would arrive at Daretown, throw down our books and rush over to the jungle gym or swings. The high school students had to sit on the front steps until the next bus arrived to take them to the high school. The same process, in reverse, would happen at night.

Often during snowstorms, tractors would be used to pull the bus through the drifts; sometimes a snowplow in the area would be diverted to go ahead of the bus. One night, because of a particularly bad blizzard, we didn't get home until almost nine P.M. It was a great adventure, and we drove our parents nuts by constantly telling the story of the storm and how we almost didn't make it out alive. Of course, we never were in any danger.

Now kids go to school before Labor Day and stay well into June. They have so much going for them with computers, qualified teachers and state of the art facilities. Not only do many schools have music and art, but they also teach languages in the lower levels. I would have been happy with just a good English teacher. Often today I kid people and say that English is my second language.

But no matter how many computers they have they will never have that story of your school bus being pulled through the blizzard by tractors.

A Storm Named Hazel

I woke up this morning and it was forty-six degrees outside. It almost feels like the first real day of autumn, with brisk cool winds blowing out of the northwest. Sweaters are required and the cats are snuggled even deeper into the blankets. The deer had a forlorn look this morning as they realized that the harsh winter months aren't too far away and they had better fatten up quickly. The late born fawns have a lot of work to do to prepare for their long journey this winter. I worry about them.

The highlight of this week was my birthday, marking the success of having made it sixty-one years. My friends from the city, worried about the caliber of celebration possible in Turkey Hollow, went to Whole Foods and drove up an entire birthday lunch last weekend. It was a CARE package done with style worthy of a gay man. The weather was still warm, and they served a spectacular meal and even cleaned up. They didn't forget that my favorite cake was coconut, and it was so sinfully good that it could qualify for confession.

I am a deep believer in birthdays. Having had so many friends die from HIV/AIDS, I think it is crucial that we celebrate life. Those of us who have gone through the epidemic understand that to be still standing after all this time is a huge victory and indeed a cause for great celebration. Will, Juan, Kevin and Jim knew just how to make it a perfect birthday, and I was glowing from the experience all week.

Now, the big news this time of year is hurricanes. Hardly anyone doesn't take them seriously anymore after Katrina, Wilma and Rita. We all know the impact and understand that we will increasingly face more intense storms during the coming years because of global warming. As on cue, Hurricane Dean is making its way towards either Mexico or Texas with 150 miles-per-hour winds. Every season, as the super storms start, I think back to when I was eight and my family's experience with Hurricane Hazel in 1954.

You don't hear much about Hurricane Hazel from weather historians but it was one of the worst storms ever to hit the east coast and especially the mid-Atlantic states. In fact, that damn storm stayed so strong for so long after it traveled inland, that it ended up being the worst hurricane to ever hit Canada. She came ashore on the North Carolina/South Carolina border with winds of 140 miles-per-hour and rapidly headed north, passing just west of Washington, D.C. and up through the east side of the Appalachian mountains.

Hurricane Hazel was a monster hurricane and wind gusts over

100 miles-per-hour were felt 100 or so miles inland and all the way to the coast, including New York and New Jersey.

Back then there was no Weather Channel, sexy weathermen standing in the rain and wind along the coast, no weather satellites, and not even weather radar. There was minimum warning and it was usually something like, "Conditions could be bad and get worse." You sort of had to make judgments based on instinct, animals and the sky.

Grandpa Grove and Dad knew a bad one was coming, and I remember all of us literally running around preparing all day long. At eight years old, I think my major contributions were small but not insignificant since everyone had their tasks. On Mr. Seabrook's farm, we took the steel bodied trucks and backed them into the barns and shops so they wouldn't blow over. We took every lose object we could find and put them inside. Mom baked as fast as she could so we would have the food if the electricity went out and the schools were let out early.

As a child, this was all very exciting to me. I remember that late in the afternoon ominous clouds started to swirl in the sky. It was like looking into the heavens with a kaleidoscope. The house we lived in was surrounded by huge thirty to forty foot pine trees. As the storm started to hit the five of us gathered in our living room. At first we were all filled with the energy of anticipation of an unknown danger heading our way. Mom and Dad put on the assured front that is required of parents in times of danger, though all the kids could sense their fear and nervousness.

As the winds started to get stronger and more violent, we fled into the front room where we thought we would be safer. The howling wind was unforgettable. Mid-way through the storm, our neighbors from across the field, the Husters, pounded on the door seeking shelter since they thought their house was going to be blown away. The room was filled and we huddled as we heard trees blowing down within feet of the house, the roofs being blown off small farm buildings and the ceaseless creaking of the house swaying in the wind.

The next morning, we walked out into our yard and it was filled with fallen trees. Several small farm buildings had lost their roofs and there was significant damage on all the local farms. Although the hurricane killed ninety in the US, all made it safely through the storm in our area. It is an experience you never forget. Hurricane Hazel is etched into the minds of my family.

That old gal Hazel is listed among the thirty most damaging hurricanes ever to hit the US and among the twenty most deadly. For my family, it was "the hurricane" and we'll always remember that night in the front room, huddling together among the sounds and fury of a mighty storm.

Short of Money

Even Turkey Hollow was not spared the absolute terror that grips the stomach when serious financial woes ram into our lives. Most often it is the fear of a bad illness, loss of a job or that someone has to be sent to recovery. Our families and neighbors can be a huge comfort—steady rocks for us to cling to in difficult times. But what happens when everyone is short of money? This week the calm of the fall air in the Hollow was violently intruded upon by the news that our government and financial institutions had seriously lost the trust of the American people.

As one went to town and faced the neighbors, fear was on everyone's face. The word "Depression" was whispered between friends. There was that very tentative "how're you doing?" exchanged by friends and not really wanting to know the answer. There are a lot of people who have second homes in the Hollow who work on Wall Street, and we were eager for them to arrive for the weekend to be sure they were okay from the brutal ride that was taking place in the markets all week long. There was a general acknowledgement that the situation was likely to get worse, even if it temporarily got better.

Often I heard from the farmers and workers, "How in the hell did we get to the position where we have to turn to China to bail us out? What has happened to America?" Economic insecurity is one of the greatest fears that can exist within an individual or a family. Not having money to buy food, gas to get to work, pay the doctor bills or save your home from foreclosure takes a toll that we can't possibly overestimate.

These kind of times unfortunately bring back very difficult moments from our past, when we had to witness our parents (or grandparents) being torn apart as they struggled to meet the basics. One of my most difficult memories is the time Dad came home to tell Mom that there wasn't going to be a check from Seabrook Farms as Mr. Seabrook had promised. I will never forget the look of total fear coming over my mother's face and this amazingly strong woman ran out of the house, across the fields to the hedgerow and sobbed at the news. One doesn't forget those moments when the powerful are suddenly weak and vulnerable.

My parents always had a struggle. Dad worked eighteen hours a day, especially in the summer, and Mom worked at Wheaton's Glass or the John Deere dealer to get the funds to make ends meet for us kids. My sister and I often discuss how we now remember at one point there were only two dresses in my mother's closet. Hand me down clothes were commonplace in our house. My mother could make food stretch—she'd take a little hamburger and make hamburger gravy with onions and pour it over a slice of white bread. In the summer, our table was plentiful since we would go into the fields each day and get our meals of tomatoes, corn, peas, and so on. Often we would have baked tomatoes or tomato gravy over white bread.

Now, don't get me wrong. My parents gave us kids a wonderful childhood in the country. They learned to take a little, make a lot, and have fun doing it. But I was totally aware all the time how they quietly struggled financially. They never really got that break, and when Seabrook Farms was done with Dad, they just let him go after a lifetime of helping them build their massive farm. He was devastated and never really recovered from that blow. He actually thought that giving his life to them meant they cared for him. That after all those years they had some sort of partnership.

So as the news hit this week and all those hard working people were laid off at Lehman Brothers, Hewlett-Packard, and so many other places, I couldn't help but think of the pain Mom and Dad experienced in similar circumstance. Proud people who worked hard, served their community and loved their children who were reduced to scrambling to survive. It wasn't right then and it isn't right now.

Different People, Different Times

Driving along Two Frog Creek the other day, I noticed on the side of the road a car filled with a Muslim family taking in the beauty of the area. At first I was a little taken aback but the joy in the family's eyes reflected my own and I stopped to visit. The women were dressed in the traditional *hijab* and veil; I knew to address only the male. It was a pleasant chat and learned they were up on a drive from New York City to show their children their first view of the mountains. The women in the car held their heads down and it was hard for me to quite understand their submissiveness but I respected their choice—at least I hope it was their choice.

This area of the Catskills has historically been known as the "Borsht Belt" for its history of Jewish resorts and famous Jewish comedians performing at them. So it was all the more ironic in the middle of nowhere to be visiting with a Muslim family along the rushing creek. I suggested some drives for them from Two Frog and talked about the wildlife and saw the excitement in the children's eyes as I shared stories about Benny and Betty the bears. They could not hear enough, and the father chuckled at the stories. Soon we ended our visit, I wished a safe trip and headed up the hill to the Hollow.

In many ways, I can measure my life by different people at different times. Each time a different group came to America to seek dreams of a better life, it had to fight to be assimilated and at the same time hold on to some traditions from the past. As each generation passed, more and more of the traditions were shed. Eventually after several generations struggled to become more American than the previous one, the newer generations often reached back into their past to seek those traditions once more.

When I was a child and my dad worked for Mr. Seabrook, he talked about the Dutch man who shared his knowledge of growing flowers. At the same time, a German prisoner of war camp was located in this rural area and most of the prisoners stayed after the war. They had their own little section of rural homes decorated with traditional German colors and patterns. To me, they looked liked strange little dollhouses so out of place in our rural area.

As I got a little older, Mr. Seabrook imported Jamaicans to work in the fields and to help with the pea harvest as "viners," separating the pods from the vines. They lived in the old barracks that used to hold the German prisoners, sleeping in bunk beds in a large room. The viners were located close to our home, and they would go late into the night. Often in the summer my dad would work all day. At night I could hear the hum of the viners as I attempted to go asleep but competing with the hum was the sound of Jamaicans singing in unison their songs from the island nation. The night came to be for me a place of exotic sounds as I drifted off into sleep.

Soon the Jamaicans literally found a way to escape those depressing barracks or were sent home at the end of the season, and they were replaced by Puerto Ricans who poured into South Jersey in the 1950s. Where the Jamaicans spoke the King's English, this was my first experience with people who knew no English. What were they saying? Where they talking about us? Where they saying bad things? Were they plotting to come in and kill our family at night? The mind of a child darts to many different places and all of them not very reasonable. The Anglo bosses grew very impatient when the workers couldn't understand the directions, deciding that if they shouted loudly somehow that would make the Spanish speakers suddenly understand English. My Aunt Evelyn actually had a Puerto Rican partner and it was a huge family scandal. Have to smile now, since in today's world no one would give it a second thought.

American life is about different people coming to these United States at different times, seeking the same things all the rest of us desire. Our history is measured by the inflow of these people, all with their own struggle to reach that dream. Just as I was taken aback initially by the Muslim family, once I engaged them, got past knee-jerk judgment, they were just another family taking their kids to see the mountains. Which is as it should be.

Life Turns with the Leaves

What a magnificent week it has been with temperatures going down into the forties at night and reaching into the seventies during the day. Just perfect. The crystal blue sky provides contrast for the leaves that are just now turning. In some spots, I have found trees already fully dressed in brilliant red or orange. This fall should be a carnival of color with dazzling displays over the next couple of weeks.

It's clear that the deer sense the approaching winter, and they are fattening up early this year. Perhaps that means snow could arrive sooner than later. There were a record number of young fawns born this spring. While they still trail their mothers everywhere, the signs of youth—their spots—are beginning to disappear. Still, they are unable to cut into the apples with their baby teeth, but it is just a matter of time before they compete with

Mom for a juicy taste.

The velvet has fallen off the male bucks impressive racks and, for three days, curls of velvet hung off each side of Attila's head. Since this occurred over Rosh Hashanah, I now assume that Attila is Jewish and I wished him the best of holidays. He seemed very pleased.

Attila has put together his own little herd that travels with him everywhere. Unfortunately, it is not a band of great warriors, but more like a band of rejects. There is "One Horn," who is as sweet as they come but has just one antler coming out of the left side of his head. Close by is "Whitetail," who appears to be half albino and is afraid of his own shadow. He is always the first to head into the forest when any unusual noise is heard. They blindly follow Attila around like a band of brothers. He tolerates no dissent and none are to touch the apples unless he gets the first one or all hell is to be paid.

The only time Attila mellows is when Kate arrives with Attila's two fawns. She quickly becomes the boss of the entire yard while Attila simply dotes on his two little babies. They run up to him and nudge him around. They lift their mouths to his to catch falling pieces of apple that he has chewed for them. One day, I looked out my window and there was the entire family looking up into my office, seemingly waiting for their family portrait. Sadly, my damn camera batteries were dead. I don't think he was pleased with my lack of preparedness.

I can't stand that hunting season is approaching and Attila could be in real danger. Old Man Keller says his folks won't touch him, but we worry about the city folks who come up for sport. I have come to accept how important venison is for some poor families up here. If they don't get a deer during the hunting season, it could impact their ability to feed their families for the winter. Last winter, I saw first hand how important it was for some young children that their dad was able to feed them by hunting.

The city folk who come to hunt, however, are really appalling. They are a cold bunch. They come with semi-automatic rifles, sit on their fat asses as locals drive the deer to them, shoot the deer, cut off their head for some trophy in some God awful room far away, and leave the meat to rot in the woods. They couldn't care less if that deer could feed a family for the winter. Some, who apparently could not shoot the side of a barn, pay the locals for the head so they can claim to their rich friends that they stalked the deer and shot it.

My land is posted and I could never hunt. One of the big crises for me growing up with my father was the fact that I refused to hunt. On my tenth birthday, I was given a twenty-eight-gauge shotgun, and it was a big deal because it meant that I was old enough to hunt with my father. But I cried because I didn't want to kill any animals. My father had a very difficult time understanding my unwillingness to hunt. The anger in our house was great and it fell to my mother to make the peace. I learned to shoot that gun, like all men in our community, but I did not have to go hunting. The only problem was that my sister Patsy was a better shot than me.

These last few weeks have been about recovery for me, too. I have had lots of time to interact with the deer and Mother Nature and observe her changes. About two weeks ago, my doctors discovered a massive tumor in my throat. After quite a bit of bad news from my very capable doctors, I finally received word, after extensive surgery, that the tumor was not cancerous. Needless to say, the uncertainty was difficult to endure. But now I not only breathe better, but I feel that I have a new lease on life.

Patsy, who has always looked after me, was my bedrock and held me together through the process. My friend Jeff sat with me while I was in intensive care for a night and was such a comfort. Numerous other friends, by phone and in person, shepherded me through the surgery, including Marylouise, Kevin, James, Jim, Jeremy and Alan.

Of course, I got a good old fashion lesson from my Turkey Hollow neighbors. The Carlson family drove me back and forth to the hospital, stood at the door as I came out of surgery and stocked my refrigerator with homemade soups, puddings and goodies. One could not possibly hope for better neighbors than I have up here on the mountain.

The week was a time of great challenge and revelation, and I have taken all the lessons to heart. I will make a complete recovery and be back to my sassy self in no time. After all, I have deer to feed, and I have to be strong to protect Attila from those hunters.

Fall Musings

The weather keeps playing tricks with us here in Turkey Hollow. After a cold spell, the temperature flirted with eighty degrees last week. Not only are the animals confused, I am, too. The good news is that the weather means more wonderful meals on the screened porch, short sleeve shirts and prolonging the changing of the leaves. Vivid colors still grace my woods.

Attila has learned a new trick, and I am not thrilled. When I sleep late into the morning, which is rare, he has to wait for apples. Unfortunately, he knows where I sleep in the house, and instead of waiting in the backyard, he will come to my bedroom window. He snorts and stamps his hoofs until I wake up. I roll over and say, "Damn you, Attila. Do you want your apples?" He immediately runs to the backyard and waits until I make my grand appearance.

Sleeping late no longer seems to be an option in my household.

There is nothing like sleeping with the windows open on a crisp fall night. While the sheets are cold, the comforter warms the bed. Once settled, the cats claim ownership of their designated spots. Often, there is a tug of war between us. I find myself clinging to the edge of the bed as they stretch crossways, totally comfortable.

This past week, as I sat on the porch watching the sun set and the stars take the sky, the cares of the world seemed very far away. It's sometimes hard to understand why we give our beautiful planet so little respect. Our teenagers are dying in an unjust and useless war far from our shores, and others are denied the peace and beauty that I am granted as I sit in the silent night air. Nature is just magical, and I am totally in awe of it up here in Turkey Hollow.

In my childhood days, I would walk into the woods near our home, build forts, catch frogs and build huge piles of leaves, which I would jump into from the trees. There was an enormous freedom being a young child alone in the woods. The entire world seemed to be my playground. Climbing to the top of the trees, I could see forever. The fallen trees had huge canopies of vines over them. Crawling underneath the green vines I created a secret room that became my own little private hideaway. When the leaves changed, I would lie on my back and stare through the colors. The fall leaves transfixed me with their beauty.

Dreams came easy in such places. There was nothing I couldn't imagine doing and everything seemed possible. Watching the clouds race above the leaves, my mind would transport me to far away places. I so badly wanted to see the world.

Dreams still come easy to me. Somehow the fall always makes it easier for me to dream. And what are dreams but a vehicle to make the impossible possible?

Thoughts on the Transgender Issue

It can be frustrating to witness the same old battles being fought over again, changed only by the players involved.

There is a movement afoot in the LGBT community to exclude transgender people from the ENDA civil rights legislation.

I have also reflected on these recent developments, and I feel strongly that it is dishonest to practice intolerance in order to advance equality. Imagine if the 1963 Civil Rights Act had excluded all African Americans without a college education. At the end of the day, what's the difference?

For more than thirty years, I have been involved in the struggle for LGBT rights. During these three decades, I have fought that battle side by side with transgender people. They have brought talent, wisdom, insight, energy and even humor to an often-uphill battle. My own cousin Rebecca became Frank and is living a fulfilled life. I am so proud of him and his courage to embrace his own journey and to live his life honestly. Now, some want to exclude transgender people from our community because they make others uncomfortable politically. That is just not acceptable to me.

The LGBT community worked hard to build an enduring coalition. There was even a time when lesbians and gay men wouldn't work together. Several decades ago, many gay men held onto misogynous attitudes towards women and many feminist separatists, having been burned working with men, had no desire to attempt to do so again.

The Municipal Elections Committee of Los Angeles (MECLA), the first political PAC in the history of the LGBT community, was formed by mostly gay men, including myself. When Diane Abbitt and Roberta Bennett became the first female leaders in the organization, they insisted that the Board of Directors consist of equal numbers of women and men, with both female and male co-chairs. The angry battle over the proposal was brutal. However, a group of enlightened men and women led MECLA to become the community's first gender-neutral political organization. It was because of that victory that MECLA went on to become one of the more powerful political organizations of the 1980s.

By the time the AIDS epidemic emerged, lesbians and gay men had learned to work closely together and many lesbians had emerged as leaders in the community. Women like Torie Osborn, Lori Jean, Elizabeth Birch, Hillary Rosen, Pat Denslow, Urvashi Vaid, Jean O'Leary and so many others became some of our community's greatest champions. All the while, they supported gay men in their struggle against HIV/AIDS. I can't imagine we would be where we are today without their spectacular leadership.

With this experience in mind, I feel that gays and lesbians need to embrace the transgender community, not push it away. Transgender people will continue to bring great gifts to our community and make it stronger, but only if we can get past our prejudices. Many talented leaders and powerful artists will continue to arise from this community. More than any other group in our coalition, they experience more hate crimes, more discrimination and more anger. Now is the time to rally around them, as they have for us, not abandon them for a political victory.

Vietnam Moratorium

The first frost hit this morning and it is a clear, crisp day. The fall leaves have passed their peak, and they are beginning to fall off the trees. With the vegetation thinning, I can now see deep into the woods and watch the deer wind their way down from the mountaintop.

It was just such a day on October 15, 1969 that the Vietnam Moratorium took place and more than two million people stopped work, school or daily routines to protest the war in Vietnam. Interestingly, when I think back to those days, I tend to remember the glorious times and forget the fear. It is important to remember both.

The idea for a nationwide moratorium against the war originated with Massachusetts businessman Jerome Grossman. My friend Sam Brown picked up on Grossman's idea, where the nation would stop "business as usual" for a day to discuss the Vietnam War. Sam, who was a leader in the 1968 McCarthy for President movement, contacted champion college swimmer David Hawk, who was indicted for resisting the draft, Marge Sklencar, a brilliant field organizer at Mundelein College, and myself to join him in creating the Vietnam Moratorium. Sam had raised enough money from his contacts at Harvard to open a small office in late March with barely a phone line for each of us. We had to bring the whole thing together in six and a half months.

Looking back now, I wonder what in the world were we thinking. We were four young people, with a small office, telling the press that we were going to launch the largest anti-war protest ever. We had almost no money in the bank, and we weren't quite sure how we would even pay our rent and bills. In our first week, we were sitting around on the floor, since we had no chairs yet, and Marge said, "What a way to go broke. We'll never see a paycheck!" Sam, laughing, quickly corrected Marge and said, "Marge, that is not true. We have enough for a month."

With the help of some great volunteers, we proceeded to nail down endorsements from other peace groups, political leaders, labor leaders and educational institutions. Entertainers like Shirley MacLaine and Paul Newman gave us their support and time. By late June we were ready to go public and the four of us walked to our press conference around the corner to announce our plans for October 15th and all of our thousands of endorsements. I remember vividly our conversation.

"This is really crazy," Hawk exclaimed. "Four kids about to enter a room and tell the national press that we are going to bring the nation to a halt."

"Well, it's our turn," I answered. "All the last two presidents have done is to succeed in ripping this nation apart. What the hell, we can't do any worse."

Sam laughed and said, "We are going to kick their asses today."

"Let's hope they don't kick ours!" Marge shot back.

The response was incredible, however, and the event took off with unbelievable momentum, captivating the nation. In July, I drove across the nation with my friends Dan MacIntosh and Rick Sterns in an old V.W. Bug convertible covered in peace stickers to organize support. In September, Sam and I had a long meeting with legendary United Automobile Workers leader Walter Reuther. I was in awe of this great man. Accepting great political risk to his own personal position, he promised to make his national union the first to come out against the war and endorse the Moratorium.

By September, the Moratorium had taken a life on of its own. More than 7,000 communities, colleges and organizations had pledged to conduct events in their communities and institutions. More than 400 colleges and universities agreed to suspend classes that day and to spend the day focused on the War in Vietnam. Hundreds of volunteers now crowded our three floor offices. The international media jammed our press conferences. *Newsweek* wrote, "Originally, October 15th was to have been a campus-oriented protest involving a moratorium on normal academic activities. But it has quickly spread beyond the campus. And, if everything goes according to the evolving plans, the combination of scheduled events could well turn into the broadest and most spectacular anti-war protest in American history."

Finally that day arrived. At midnight, I joined thousands sitting on the steps of the Capitol and we read the names of the war dead.

Those names ricocheted off the side of the Capitol into the night. The following morning at the Vietnam Moratorium, Marylouise Oates, with great professionalism, kept hundreds of journalists at bay until the first reports came in from around the country on our success. Pulitzer Prize-winning columnist Mary McGrory attempted to sneak by Marylouise with a picnic basket, claiming she had lunch for the four of us and thus gain an exclusive. But Marylouise caught her, seized the basket for us and put her back in the pressroom.

The reports poured in and thousands of communities around the country were holding marches, reading the names of the war dead, ringing bells, leaving classrooms, wearing black arm bands to work, holding vigils, filling religious institutions with people praying and carrying candles for the dead. It surpassed our own expectations, and the *Cleveland Plain Dealer* captured it all with a banner headline that proclaimed, "Millions Protest War."

At the end of the day, Sam and Hawk hit the late-night television shows, while Marge did a series of radio interviews. Because I was closeted and afraid to be visible, I held down the headquarters. By late that evening, it was almost over and the last reports were coming in from the West Coast. The headquarters had mostly emptied, and I had changed into my cowboy boots, tight jeans and cowboy hat. Lying down on the sofa in the office, I pulled out my harmonica and started playing "We Shall Overcome."

Getting Arrested

Reading about the recent arrests of demonstrators in Washington, D.C. against "Don't Ask, Don't Tell" brought back memories of my own political arrests over the years. Getting arrested is never pleasant, especially if you're claustrophobic like me. Hell, I can't even sit in the back seat of a two-door car let alone rest comfortably in a room consisting of a toilet, bars, and twenty other people. Now, those of us who have been "repeat offenders" and long-term practitioners of Gandhian civil disobedience tend to know jailhouse etiquette. These acquired skills always come in handy to assist "newcomers" who love the handcuffs in public but aren't quite prepared for the reality of even a day behind bars.

Going to jail can be a very effective strategy in raising public awareness in an epic struggle for freedom. The arrest advances an issue and the sacrifice is rewarded with progress in a number of different ways. Other times I have gone to jail simply to "give witness" against a great evil. The concept is that you are not likely to change minds, but the evil is so powerful you give witness against it. For example, after the start of the Iraq War, getting arrested was not going to end the war but enabled me to give witness against it by my sacrifice.

There is not a time that I have wanted to go to jail, been comfortable in jail or wanted to stay in jail. The experience is not a picnic, and the accommodations are certainly not the Four Seasons. Despite my dark memories of some of these experiences (and trust me there were dark ones), I'm usually reminded of those moments that still make me smile or laugh.

When Nixon invaded Cambodia at the end of April in 1970, there was a storm of protests around the country with over 400 universities having to shut their doors due to massive demonstrations. A group of us who had been active in organizing the national protests against the war and a large number of the clergy decided to get arrested in front of the White House. Everything went as planned but the cops were a little rough because tensions were high in the nation. However, what was unique to that experience was Betty Anne Ottinger, wife of Congressman Richard Ottinger. coming down to the jail to bail us out. Watching Betty Anne negotiate with the police was very funny.

When the International AIDS Conference was held in Washington, D.C., sixty-four LGBT leaders and HIV/AIDS activists decided to get arrested in front of the White House. Among those arrested were Leonard Matlovich, Ginny Apuzzo, Rev. Troy Perry, Jim Foster, Dan Bradley, Jean O'Leary and Sean Strub. At that time Pennsylvania Avenue (the nation's Main Street) was still open to traffic in front of the President's residence. Blocking the street, we awaited our arrests. Pouring out of the police transports were literally over a hundred cops wearing riot gear and, most importantly, long yellow gloves to protect them from even touching us for fear of HIV/AIDS. Never to be trumped by the cops, we all started chanting, "Your gloves don't match your shoes." In the process, we drew the attention of the press to this insult, and the gloves quickly disappeared from police practice.

When President Clinton decided to hide behind "Don't Ask, Don't Tell," twenty to thirty of us (about two-thirds from Los Angeles) decided to get arrested in front of the White House in protest. Because of my friendship with the President we drew a little more press than normal. Our arrests were a huge story. As we got arrested, the police removed our belts and shoelaces before loading us into the "wagon." As this momentous event was taking place, all I could think was that my pants were going to fall down to my ankles—and I was commando. How stupid of me! As he placed me into the wagon, an officer apologized for arresting me and pointed out that his brother was gay. I asked him if he could run the siren when we left to remind the people in the White House we were out here. He said it wasn't allowed. Nevertheless, as we pulled away, the siren blared loud and clear for freedom.

Taken to jail, the men were put in one cell and the women in another down the hall. We figured out that if we stood on a bench and yelled into a vent we could send messages back and forth between the two cells. We used every bad movie line about being in the lockup you can imagine. We laughed until tears filled our eyes. In the process, I figured a way to get out of my cuffs and realized that in the men's cell I was suddenly cellblock boss. Ah, the sweet smell of power and the helplessness of my fellow inmates. This was the arrest where current West Hollywood Mayor John

Duran, when being booked, finger printed, and having a mug shot taken, was asked by the booking Sergeant if John went by any other alias. Without missing a beat the future mayor looked the Sergeant in the eyes and said in a masculine voice, "Yeah, I sometimes go by Mary." We were rolling with laughter in the cell at the stricken look on the officer's face as he said, "Oh God, it's going to be a very long day, isn't it?"

Since our arrests all those years ago, over 14,000 LGBT soldiers have been drummed out of the military in one massive witchhunt. My hat is off to those who continue to get arrested in protest of DADT, to the courage of all those within the military who have courageously faced their oppressors and to a LGBT community that refuses to give up.

Citizen Paul Newman

One of Hollywood's greatest legends, Paul Newman, has died of cancer. Much will be made—and should be made—of his considerable talent and long list of box office hits. Films such as *The Hustler*, *Hud*, *Cool Hand Luke*, *Butch Cassidy and the Sundance Kid*, *The Sting*, and *The Verdict* remain classics. Many of the articles will note that he was one of the most generous stars in the entertainment industry. The much-lauded actor developed a line of food products called Newman's Own, and every cent of the profits went to support a camp for disabled children in Connecticut. Few stars have given so much to so many.

However, there is a side of Paul Newman that has received very little attention, despite the fact that it's equally as important as his philanthropy. Fortunately for me, I was able to experience that side first hand at least three times in my life. Newman was an outstanding citizen. He participated in the political process to the fullest and gave of his time and energy to numerous campaigns, causes, and fights for justice. He was totally fearless, often risking his career by taking public stands on difficult and unpopular issues. To those of us who worked with him on making the world a safer place, he was thoughtful, kind and caring. He treated as peers with deep respect—and a wicked sense of humor.

Just as Newman was riding on a crest of success from his earlier movies, he became involved in the civil rights struggles of the 1960s. He not only leant his name but also called upon other entertainers personally to get involved in marches and fund raising events. He was also instrumental in facilitating the bottom line by getting his compatriots in Hollywood to write checks. That same level of involvement carried over into opposition of the Vietnam War. In 1968, mostly through the efforts of a Connecticut neighbor, Anne Wexler, Newman played a major role in the campaign of Senator Eugene McCarthy. The senator's campaign was the key avenue for citizens wishing to express their opposition to the war. Newman traveled with the senator from one end of the country to the other, speaking out against the war.

During this campaign, I was a young man of twenty-two, working day and night to get McCarthy the Democratic nomination for president. In fact, there were so many young people working for the senator, we became known as the "Children's Crusade." This was the first time I met Mr. Newman. He paid a visit to one of the headquarters and spent time going from desk to desk, asking each of us what was going on and how we were hanging in there considering the very rough politics of the 1960s. We were awestruck, not only by his graciousness and charisma, but also by his genuine concern. He left an unforgettable impression on every one of us in the room.

After the brutal Chicago Democratic Convention of 1968, Newman, unlike so many others, was not discouraged by the turn of events. Instead, he became more focused. In 1970, the increasingly international star made a personal crusade to help the peace campaign of Joseph Duffy in Connecticut. Their friendship was to last a lifetime.

A more intimate interaction with Newman took place in 1969, when my friends and I launched the National Vietnam Moratorium against the war. Not surprisingly, Newman was right there to support this effort and the massive march of 600,000 that took place on October 15th. He also brought Robert Redford and Jon Voight to Washington, D.C. for a meeting with the Moratorium's organizers to discuss how Hollywood could become more involved. The meeting took place in Newman's hotel room and lasted several hours. I have to admit to being star struck, but that reaction was quickly placed on the back burner as Newman not only put us at ease but, more importantly, got down to the fine details on how to stop the war. His expansive knowledge on foreign affairs was breathtaking.

Off and on over the next years, I had various opportunities to work with Mr. Newman, but I shall always remember him most fondly for being especially instrumental in helping me through a very difficult time. In 1986, I conceived an effort called the Great Peace March Across America. While many brave and amazing individuals worked on this plan, it was to be my most difficult and bitter political—as well as personal—failure. The vision was to walk thousands across America to bring a halt to the spread of nuclear weapons that were endangering the world. Despite extraordinary public support at the beginning—including support from Newman—the March began to collapse like a house of cards because of my ego and inability to implement good leadership. The failure of the well-meaning project was front-page news around the world and much of the negative publicity focused on my failed leadership.

In the middle of this disastrous moment, Newman telephoned. He said he wanted me to know he was concerned about me, said he wished more people would take chances like I had and promised me things would get better. He had one simple request: he asked that I never become so discouraged that I stopped attempting to create change, find justice and promote peace. I will never ever forget that call.

America has lost not only a great actor, it also lost one of its finest citizens. Paul Newman will be missed by so many. Our lives may be paler because of his passing, but our nation is more robust, more informed and more humane because of his passion.

Our Neighbors and our Wounded

As we reach toward the end of October, the weather at times is more like August. The good news is that the colorful leaves have stayed around longer than usual. For over a month now the leaves have given us a daily display of magnificent colors. As the sun comes up in the morning, the gold leaves especially shine like they belong in Fort Knox.

After an absence of almost four weeks, one of my favorite deer returns to the Hollow. One Horn showed up in the back yard with a silly grin. Old Man Keller says often the does will drive a male out of the area so they won't inbreed with each other. He was not surprised that One Horn had disappeared. He seemed more surprised that he dared to show up again.

With Old Man Keller, the Carlsons, and so many others, I am reminded on a daily basis what wonderful neighbors occupy the

Turkey Hollow area. Americans have always had a way of usually being great neighbors. It is almost an American virtue that seems to have been developed over the years from when pioneers had to depend on each other for company, shared worked and protection.

That is why I am disappointed how little attention Americans are paying our wounded soldiers as they come home from Iraq. Our service members are our family and neighbors. No matter what anyone thinks of the Iraq War, these citizens served us with bravery and courage. Right now we are nearing 30,000 of our neighbors who are returning severely wounded from this horrible war. That doesn't count those with serious mental trauma from repeated tours of duty. Many of our sons and daughters are missing limbs and a large number have neurological disorders from severe head injuries.

In the media, with the exception of a story here and there, they seem to be forgotten. After all, they most likely think, once you have done one "missing limb" story what is the new "angle"? So our wounded neighbors and family members are almost "warehoused" out of sight and rarely heard from. I know when they return to their neighborhoods that Americans will be there for them. But many will not be able to return home for quite some time due to the severity of their wounds.

We owe our sons and daughters more than waiting for their return safely to their hometowns. This nation should be focused on providing these brave citizens the best of care, constant reminders of our gratitude for their service, honored on a daily basis and to be sure they know we are there for them.

The American spirit of taking care of our own has always been powerful. We are losing this virtue as our wounded return. They are a reminder of the war that none of us are able to end. They remind us of our powerlessness and the awful truth of Iraq. We have to get past that and just simply be good neighbors like the kind we find in Turkey Hollow.

I know we can do it.

"Mr. Mixner Goes to Oxford"

The Hollow is a more peaceful place these days since the second home people have boarded up, the tourists have disappeared and the summer camps have closed. It is my favorite time of year, knowing I can drive into town and the people who are passing me on DeBruce Road actually might be neighbors and friends.

Benny and Betty the bears have picked out their abode for the winter or at least have narrowed down the possibilities. The deer are frantically fattening up to get through what old-timers say will be a tough winter, based on forecasts and nature's signs. The migratory birds have headed south and left us with the more hardy flocks. Most of the smaller animals have moved down the mountain and into the valley where it is easier to survive the winter. By the time the sun appears over one peak and settles at the end of the day behind the other peak it means days with very little light.

For me, I am making my preparations for winter, including getting the snow blower running, having my car checked for winter, new snow shovels, fresh cut firewood, planting that needs to be done before the ground freezes and getting salt for when the sidewalks ice up.

But the next week will be preparing to head to Oxford University in England to speak. Now this is a big deal for me.

Growing up in rural America, names like Oxford, Harvard, and Yale were places that folks like us only got to visit and take pictures of. In our minds, you had to be rich and well connected to gain admission to the hallowed halls. If not, then you had to be person with almost mythological talent to mix with the privileged. When I first became involved with the civil rights and anti-war movements in the sixties, it seemed to be populated with people who attended Ivy League schools. Just learning that they were from those universities elevated them in my eyes. Sometimes they didn't deserve that respect, but at the time my own self-esteem deemed it necessary.

Over the years, that misperception vanished and the reality that the attendees of those places of knowledge were, as my father would say, "People who had to put their pants on one leg at a time." I even was asked to speak at some of these American institutions. As I read to make up for my lack of a college degree, eventually I realized that I even had more awareness on some issues. It was a good feeling.

In 1970, I went to Oxford University to visit my friend Bill Clinton who was a Rhodes Scholar at the time. He was sharing a house with Strobe Talbort who was secretly in his room translating

Nikita Khrushchev's memoirs. Khrushchev was Premier of the Soviet Union through most of the 1950s and early 1960s, and Strobe had smuggled his memoirs out. What an exciting time it was for me to be in their home. I walked through the Deer Meadows at Oxford and roamed the old edifices. Admittedly, I was intimidated, but I fell in love with the place.

So imagine my surprise, when out of the blue, came an invitation to participate in a debate in the historic Oxford Union. Next week, I will be debating "Change vs. Experience." At first, I was scared by the idea but now I relish it.

The Union was founded in 1823 and eleven British Prime Ministers have been members. Presidents Carter, Nixon and Reagan have spoken to students there over the years. W.B Yeats, the Dalai Lama, Mother Teresa, Prime Minister George and Desmond Tutu have shared knowledge in the building. I look forward to taking my place and savoring every moment. What comes out of my mouth will just have to do.

Downning, Oxford and Home

Well, there's no place like home. That old adage happens to be true. After traveling to Great Britain and experiencing a memorable week, I loved returning to my Turkey Hollow. There is no noise, the air is clean, the woods sparkle from a fresh rain and my own bed felt like heaven. Now that I am home, I am fully enjoying what was indeed a good week, and I am able to sit back and savor the experience.

Early in the week, I posted an article that appeared in Britain about a lunch in my honor at 10 Downing Street. As a child, if you told me that I would be breaking bread in the State Dining room of the British Prime Minister, I would have laughed you out of my neck of the woods. My mom used to call them her "pinch me" moments. What made the occasion so much more special was that for the first time in England's noble history members of the LGBT community were invited to lunch in that very dining room. It speaks volumes about the type of people who happen to live at 10 Downing Street. Prime Minister Brown (who was busy dealing with the financial crisis) and Ms. Brown happen to live their lives the way they want to see the world. If only the world was as gracious, thoughtful and kind as Sarah Brown then we would live in a special place.

No matter what happens in the British elections the next time around, Prime Minister and Ms. Brown will be known for their intellect and for calmly approaching this economic crisis with innovative solutions. History will generously embrace their lives and their work. The British Isles are fortunate to have them at this critical time in the world.

From Downing I headed to Oxford to debate at the Oxford Union. Oxford for me was a much more fearful place than Downing. The Oxford Union has existed for hundreds of years and some of the best minds have debated there. In addition, I know there is no mind like brilliant young minds, and I was about to engage them in debate. The ritual of the debate is steeped in tradition and pomp and circumstance. I met with young student leaders before the debate over dinner in the splendor of the Union's library building. With the leaders dressed in their white/black tie around a U-shaped table, toasts were made to the Queen, God, country and Oxford. I think if they could have gotten away with it, Oxford would have come first.

The students gave me great hope as they were filled with passion about our times, eager for new knowledge, and were respectful. My debate team consisted of two young students and myself advocating the change side and we plotted over dinner.

Both of these young men were thrilled about Obama and the symbolism he represents of "a torch being passed to a new generation."

From dinner we proceeded in procession to the Oxford Union debate chambers that have existed for hundreds of years. The beautiful stone building is almost oval in shape, and the inside reminded me of Shakespeare's Globe Theater. The throne-like chairs for the leaders of the Union are at the far end and there are benches on each side for the debaters. The rest of the downstairs was filled with space for the audience. A balcony encircled the space with people leaning over watching the "show." A person announced the arrival of the procession with clapped hands, and we entered a building that was packed with students. So many showed up this evening they had to turn people away. Looking up as I entered, my breath was taken away.

The debate was classic, and both sides of the issue presented challenging points with wit, knowledge and passion. In the end, the audience votes on who won by walking through one of two doors to express their opinion on the evening. The "change team" won by one of the largest margins in Oxford's history. I was one relieved guy.

So from the heady atmosphere of Downing Street and Oxford, I return to Turkey Hollow, which has a way to immediately make you humble in the presence of God's magnificent beauty. But even nature will take a few days to bring me back to earth.

Halloween

Well, pumpkins are carved, corn stalks are piled high, gourds adorn dining room tables and decorations hang from the houses of Turkey Hollow. As the frost hints of the approaching winter, Halloween is the last opportunity for many to celebrate outdoors with children trick-or-treating and massive street parties in almost every major city in the nation.

How far we have come from the days when I was a young man in Elmer. The night before Halloween was also known back then as "Mischief Night," and the old-timers would captivate us with stories of practical jokes, like the time one took apart a tractor and put it back together on a farmer's roof or the time another kidnapped a neighbor's outhouse, placing it squarely in the local traffic circle. For my generation, the event mostly meant soaping people's car windows and leaving farm equipment or other articles in their front yards—pranks that required little imagination and even less energy.

Up until the fifth grade, we all dressed up for Halloween and paraded around the school. We would walk through the sixth, seventh and eighth grade classrooms and the older students would laugh and point. We thought they were laughing at our clever costumes until we got to those grades ourselves.

For some reason, I was one of those students who was afraid to take a costume to class. I have no idea if it was the fear of the laughter or fear of falling in love with drag and revealing my gayness. Whatever the reason, it has carried through to this day. However, I do think that I would make a magnificent Kate Smith; I'd lip-sync "God Bless America" in a black dress with a handkerchief tucked into my ample front. But alas, the fear of compromising photographs circulating the Internet has kept me from that fantasy.

When I came out of the closet, Halloween was like a national holiday in the LGBT community. Costumes would be worked on for months, and some would be simply spectacular in their grandeur and creativity. I was in awe of the joy, celebration and freedom of Halloween during my first few years in West Hollywood. In those days, the Los Angeles Sheriff's Department came out in full force and aggressively and judgmentally attempted to keep us on the sidewalks and out of the street. But no one was going to ruin our holiday and as the evening wore on, the streets became filled with mostly gays and lesbians fulfilling fantasies and celebrating wildly what had become our own unique holiday.

Today, West Hollywood hosts about a half a million people on Halloween, and there are as many straights as gays. Stages take over Santa Monica Boulevard and there are as many on-lookers as costumed participants. Many members of the LGBT community mourn the fact that Halloween celebrations, such as the one in West Hollywood, have become so mainstream. To me, these celebrations are just another wonderful gift and celebration that our community has offered to the world.

In Turkey Hollow, houses are decorated with orange lights and huge, inflatable goblins sit in front yards. Halloween decorations now seem to rival the lighting of houses during Christmas and the winter holidays. In our major cities, some Halloween festivals surpass even Mardi Gras in attendance, with costume contests, bands playing on temporary street stages, community parades, and literally hundreds of thousands of participants and spectators. In some ways, America seems to have developed one long holiday from Halloween to New Year's Eve.

That can't be all bad.

Crashing to Earth

Ever since the government's announcement that a huge, lumbering "spy satellite" had run out of power and was due to come hurtling to earth, the denizens of Turkey Hollow had been hoping for the best—that it would crash in our woods. Think of the excitement. Think of the notoriety. Think of the big bucks.

We knew that the 20,000-pound piece of crippled space junk (zippily named "USA 193") contained the toxic chemical Hydrazine in its fuel, which could harm anyone coming into contact with it. We also were aware that the satellite carried a bunch of hush-hush "state secrets." And we read all about the griping of other nations, most notably China, that this maneuver may just be a cover for illegally testing missiles. But for us, those wonky fine-points paled with the realization that if the hunk of NASA metal would just fall within our city limits, then Turkey

Hollow would have a long-overdue economic shot in the arm. The added attraction of being able to mercilessly tease the Pentagon about having access to their famous "secrets" made us all the more giddy.

Within days, my friend Steven and I had the full-on economic revival of Turkey Hollow all figured out. Even Livingston Manor, the big city in the area, is struggling in this recession. People all around us are disenfranchised or disillusioned in one way or another. So we decided it was our moral obligation to do anything we could do to help our local economy. Our plan was massive, extensively researched and comprehensively detailed. We also Xeroxed and circulated nifty "X-Marks-the-Spot" maps for townspeople to bet odds on where the crippled satellite might come crashing to earth as it split up into what one NASA scientist opined would be "1,000,000 pieces of debris." Woo-hoo! That's all we needed to hear.

First off, we would enlist Old Man Keller, who we all know can do anything. Not only would Mr. Keller protect us from the toxic chemicals, most likely he would also develop a renewable use for them. Before long, happy townspeople would be using the recycled hazardous waste as lighter fluid to start wood burning stoves. Or employing a pesticide derivative to rid the countryside of encroaching chickweed. Then, en masse, we would all carry the tonnage of downed metal up to Mr. Keller's "shop" and help him cut them into pieces so we could date them and sell them on eBay as "certified spy satellite pieces."

Think of the profit to be made sending all those tiny boxes of dated space junk to P.O. boxes all around the world. Half of Turkey Hollow could be gainfully employed just packing the shipments. The tourism boom would be incredible. People would come from far and wide to see the scorched area of the woods where the satellite came to its ignominious end. Our small bed and breakfasts would be packed to capacity and the local Robin Hood Diner would have to hire on extra help to handle the curious masses.

Even more satisfying, when the tourists got bored, we would still have the entertainment value of uniformed minions of the Pentagon, along with their Beltway lawyers, darting around the frozen terrain, attempting to retrieve our new-found pirate booty. They would be holed up for months trying to negotiate down the narrow ice-encrusted dirt road out of town alone. Consider the huge financial boon for the local tow trucker, pulling black car after black car out of the side ditches. Imagine the glee of watching government bureaucrats, barking into cell phones, striving to maintain a modicum of dignity while facing the "shock and awe" of a pitiless Northeast winter.

Finally, what fun we would have exposing their secrets. The never-before-seen stats, which revealed that the Industrialized Military Complex used Energizer Bunny batteries instead of molecular solar implants. Or that the multi-million dollar satellite was intrinsically flawed from the beginning, due to the discovery of one of the Pentagon's $700 screw drivers from the rubble. Or that the craft's guidance system was actually a GM GPS system swiped from a 2006 Yukon pickup truck. We were keenly aware of what happened to whistle-blowers, but we didn't care. Duty first to the words in the Constitution.

So, in the end, the Pentagon's modified SM-3 missile not only destroyed the satellite but also shattered our collective dream. Our cash cow was shot out of the sky. To top it all, the contact blast was a disappointment—the earth didn't rumble, the heavens did not light up in a spectacular show. No bang, no boom, no ooh and ahhs like at the county fireworks display. It was all a frustrating, dispiriting dud.

Disappointed but undaunted, Steven and I have vowed to get back to the drawing boards and PowerPoint presentations to configure a new economic recovery plan for Turkey Hollow. Starting over. Back to the basics. Such is life.

Growing Up American

The town of Pole Tavern was just a circle with a grocery store, a gas station, the Pole Tavern Diner and a John Deere tractor store. Occupying one part of the circle was the Township Hall with a big, 800-pound Civil War cannon out front. Here is where my family voted. I'll never forget my dad allowing me to mark his paper ballot when he voted. I can't remember whom he directed me to vote for, but knowing his politics, I dread thinking about it now. However, it was a special moment.

Neighbors would gather, have coffee and talk about the election. The atmosphere was one of an old country store with farmers in their coveralls and boots, women in their print dresses and sensible shoes. They were all white people and very secure in their sense of being Americans. No matter many times I went to the Township Hall, they always liked to tell me about the Civil

War cannon. As a child, there were still senior citizens whose fathers had served in the War Between the States. Not many but one here and one there. We weren't that far removed from it. I remember when the last Civil War veteran died in 1956. In fact, I was fourteen when we celebrated the 100th year anniversary of that bloodbath.

There was an older gentleman named Mr. Garrison, who lived up a long farmer's lane and sat on his porch, reading the Bible. He was in his nineties when I was in grade school, and I think had been born in the 1870s. He used to tell me about his grandfather fighting in the Civil War and I was transfixed. He would say, "My grandfather said to me, 'We saved this country but at such a terrible price. God must have had a reason.'" Then Mr. Garrison would recite once more how many times he had read the Bible. In listening to his stories and others, a sense of history was passed on, and I felt part of the coming of age of a great nation.

This was a time before mass media or even private telephones. We had the old party line with eight people on it. I still can remember our phone number: ELmer 8-7066. To call outside we had to get the local operator to put us through to the next town. Without the mass intrusion of television in my early years, entertainment revolved around parades, beauty pageants and summer picnics. The church would have its events at a "private lake," so that no African Americans could swim in the water. Being a young child, it never dawned on me why we had to pay to swim in a country lake when so many others were available to swim in for free. Only later in life did I get it.

Eventually we bought a television and the world began to open up. My first real awareness of the concept of freedom was the Hungarian Revolution in 1956. I was mesmerized by the newsreel coverage of people in the streets of Budapest fighting tanks with stones. Our entire nation's heart went out to them, and I gave them my heart, too. Soon, injustice triumphed over the stones and I was devastated. However, when those refugees who captured people's hearts with their courage needed a new home, many of my neighbors were adamantly opposed to bringing them to America. They thought we didn't need any more foreigners. This was my first education on immigration and the fickle nature of public opinion.

As time flew by, I learned that African Americans could not vote, that our country was lagging behind the USSR in space exploration, and that there was no freedom nor free speech on college campuses. That America could send troops to an unjust war. This nation could ignore thousands dying of HIV/AIDS. And the toughest lesson of all was that, as a gay man, I was not free in my own nation.

Despite all these hard lessons, I remember Mr. Garrison talking about young men fighting to save the Union. Over 500,000 died and hardly a family was spared. Recently it occurred to me that my proximity to the Civil War and its legacy is part of the reason I have never given up on America. Over and over, despite the division, tensions, hate and mistrust, I have seen our country survive and stay together. As Mr. Garrison's grandfather memorably said, "God must have a reason."

November 22, 1963

Funny how a simple date has the capacity to define a generation. For my parents, the date always carried in their heart was December 7, 1941. Today's young people will most likely have September 11th as their foremost remembrance. For my generation, every time the date November 22nd appears on our calendar, we flashback to the horrific day of President Kennedy's assassination in Dallas.

That date is etched into my heart and mind. It changed the world forever and took the innocence of an entire generation. Many of us considered ourselves the "children of Kennedy." President Kennedy represented a new moment of hope in our history. He convinced us that to honor our country and to serve others in the world was a great aspiration. His grace, charm and charisma left us breathless. The concept of "Camelot" in the

White House was real. The President was the leader of a new land and, at his side was the fair lady, Jacqueline. We were optimistic and proud.

There is a cafe in the town of War, West Virginia that has a calendar on the wall permanently showing November 22, 1963. When asked about it, the older waitress simply says, "Honey, that is the day our hope died. That calendar has been like that since that day." The anniversary of his death this week, hung sadly in my mind as well.

Being a junior in high school, I was between classes when a classmate rushed up and shouted, "They shot Kennedy!" The guy was always the class clown and I didn't take him too seriously; I thought it was a horrible joke. The rumors buzzed as I settled into my next class. There was a terrible anxiety in the air. We gathered around the radio in Mr. Hickey's history class and listened to the bulletins pouring out of Dallas. A few minutes later, the dreaded announcement came over the small transistor radio, "The President of the United States is dead," followed quickly by classical music. I lost it. Soon everyone in our small high school in Woodstown, New Jersey was crying and sobbing. Most of all we were stunned, no one quite knew what to do. I was out of control and kept hitting my fist into my locker and weeping like a baby.

After a silent bus ride home, I turned on the radio and my favorite rock-n-roll station, WIBG in Philly, was playing only classical music. My parents stopped work early and came home in disbelief. We all gathered around the television set to watch the news. I saw tears in my parents' eyes. The sight was extremely rare and it scared me.

After many hours, my father broke the sad living room silence and enlisted me to ride with him to Sherman Ale's Country Store to get some groceries. The newsstand headline confirmed in the darkest and boldest of print, "PRESIDENT DEAD." Even with the massive headlines, I just couldn't believe our brilliant, young leader was gone. It wasn't possible.

My father and I returned home just as the television cut to the live feed of Air Force One's arrival at Andrews Air Force Base. My family watched in horror as the First Lady, her suit splattered with the President's blood, followed the casket of our fallen hero. Mrs. Kennedy's heartbreaking eyes confirmed that the day was, in fact, real. The band played sorrowfully while an entire world was quiet as he was placed in the hearse and taken to the White House. We knew then it was true.

Like most Americans that night, I cried myself to sleep.

Thanksgiving Memories

I'm a sucker for holidays, and I particularly look forward to the last six weeks of each year. I'm not sure if it is my imagination, but the days do seem more joyful and the nights seem to sparkle, with families gathered, houses decorated and people literally singing in the streets.

As I grew up in a small rural town in the 1950s, Thanksgiving was a big deal. Since the age of global travel had not really hit Elmer yet, all our relatives lived close by. Having completed the end-of-season harvest, people had time to visit, tell stories and catch up on chores that had been neglected during the summer growing season. The tractors had to be repaired, the barns needed to be painted and our family began to prepare for the winter snows.

Our house usually hosted a huge Thanksgiving dinner for my

mother's family. The Wednesday before Thanksgiving was always a frenzy at our home, with Mom making lemon butter, spiced peaches, pickled eggs and her delicious homemade pies. Grandpa Grove would make the "filling" (stuffing) and always put a cigar ash in it for good luck over the holiday season. While the first chill of winter would be setting in, the kids were outside attempting to get the last moments of fall play in before the weather became too harsh. The kitchen was a beehive of activity late into the night. In the dining room, a single long table would be constructed from a variety of smaller tables. There was always a kids table, and one of the more joyful moments I recall was when I graduated to the adult table.

For the kids, Thanksgiving morning was about "the game." For years, Woodstown High played its main rival, Salem, on Thanksgiving morning. Unfortunately, they beat us year after year. During my senior year, we finally smashed them in the Thanksgiving game, which made for an exciting dinner, as we could not believe we had broken the curse.

Later in the afternoon, each family arrived at our house with their favorite home-cooked dish. The house was filled with laughter as at least two dozen relatives gathered. We exchanged gossip while setting piles of food on the dining room table and another table nearby. Someone would say grace and we would dig in with a vengeance. We never ran out of food on holidays. During the rest of the year, we would often live on whatever crops were in the fields. But at Thanksgiving, the food seemed endless. Everyone gorged themselves on every kind of home-cooked delight you can imagine.

Afterwards, my Dad and Aunt Ann would do the dishes

together and the rest of us would pass out on the living room floor moaning with pain from eating too much. Our job was twofold. First we had to let our stomach's settle, so we could have leftovers that evening, and we had to listen to family storytellers talk of days and people from the past. I was riveted to the storytelling, but never let it get in the way of a second helping. We gave great reverence to our elders, especially Grandpa Grove. He would dazzle us with outrageous stories, which I always bought hook, line and sinker.

Eventually, the modern world seeped into Elmer and the tradition started to change. People moved, others passed on, and making a living of the land became tougher as technology intruded. The table became smaller and the food seemed less significant, but the spirit was still with us. For years, we tried to recreate times past and while we came close at times, the world was a different place. Storytelling was replaced with television and the food would come from a caterer.

I will always give thanks for those moments and never forget them.

Winter

Looking Into the Heavens

I live near the top of a mountain where city lights can't obstruct the spectacular scene of a clear night sky. It's a gift that comes with living here. Having lived in big cities for the last several decades, I had forgotten the splendor of stars in the night sky.

The other night after a major snowstorm, the northwest winds howled. The star-filled sky suddenly grew dark and then light again as the wind tossed puffs of clouds overhead. I watched a magical show outside my window on the fresh snow, which reflected the shadows of clouds dancing in the moon's light. The woods became my orchestra, as the trees swayed in the light, creating vivid patterns and complementing the show. Broadway has nothing on the theater of Turkey Hollow.

I shut all the lights out in the house and lit a roaring fire. Pulling my favorite chair to the window, I sat down to enjoy the view. The joy of reconnecting with the sky was overwhelming and, in that quiet moment, memories that I had long forgotten suddenly came back to me.

My mother used to sit me in her lap in the kitchen rocker and hold me in her arms. We would look out onto the moon filled sky together and she would gently rock me and softly sing:

I see the moon
The moon sees me
The moon sees somebody I want to see
So please Mr. Moon that shines on me
Shine on the one I love

I grew up in an age when space travel evolved from Saturday morning science fiction, like *Flash Gordon: The Dominion of Ming* starring Buster Crabbe (one of my first male fantasies) to real life space travel. We were a transitional generation, as the sky became a place to explore, not just dream about.

Night after night in October 1957, my entire family stood in our backyard to catch a glimpse of Sputnik, the world's first satellite raised to the heavens by the "Godless Communists." We expected that some sort of menacing evil would take over the sky. Each day our local paper, *Bridgeton Evening News*, printed a chart telling us where to look. After several nights searching the sky, we finally saw the "red menace" and it was just a tiny little light flying across the southwestern sky. This little space satellite that we were so fearful of was only the size of a basketball and weighed less than 200-pounds.

But mostly, my memories were of swimming at night in the irrigation pond and seeing millions of stars overhead. Or of thunderstorms, which we watched approach across the cornfields as they filled the night with lightening. On one winter night, the Northern Lights brilliantly filled the north sky. Mom and Dad were fascinated and it was highly unusual to see the lights that far south.

Then, as I grew older and became more of a city boy, the irrigation pond was replaced by my swimming pool in Palm Springs, where we swam naked at night. On Safari in Africa, the stars seemed so close that I felt like I could reach up and touch them and put them in my pocket. One time, a couple of us went out into the dessert and got stoned before watching meteorites fall from the August sky.

So up here in Turkey Hollow, the heavens and I have become friends again. The moon is my night-light.

A Personal Memory of Odetta

The legendary folk singer Odetta passed away this week. While not a household name, she was a major influence on singers such as Bob Dylan, Joan Baez, and even Janis Joplin. Dr. Martin Luther King, Jr. referred to her as the "The Queen of American Folk Music" and other singers honored her with the title "The Voice of the Civil Rights Movement." Her album *Odetta Sings Folk Songs* was one of the bestselling recordings of 1963, for which she received one of three Grammy nominations. She was a fixture on concert tours in the 1960s and especially on college campuses. She loved the young activists she met and influenced along the way. I was one of them.

Her death brought back deep personal memories.

In mid-1960s, I met her after a concert at Arizona State University. Because I had been organizing Hispanic garbage workers in a strike for better wages, I was led backstage after the concert for a personal visit. She was my favorite singer and I was totally star struck that I was to finally meet her. This majestic, sizable figure emerged and dressed in African garb, walked right toward me sporting a dazzling smile. She said, "This is the one, isn't it? This is the one that is helping those poor workers. I can tell from his face." With that she hugged me and whispered, almost lyrically into my ear, "We all love you for them and so many others. Don't stop with them, honey. There are so many others. You organize them, and I will sing for them." She pulled back, smiled again and asked if I would like to hear a verse or two. Several of us set around her like pupils as she strummed and sang "Oh, Freedom." I was in heaven.

She entered my life next in 1970 in Washington, D.C. The Vietnam Moratorium group was holding an event at the All Souls Unitarian Church. All Souls was literally hollowed grounds; the congregation had been militant abolitionists in the fight against slavery. One of its assistant pastors, Reverend James Reeb, was killed during the Selma Marches in 1965. It was to be a nondenominational spiritual service with prominent religious leaders and Senator Eugene McCarthy reciting poetry.

Desperate to once again hear my favorite singer in person, I contacted Odetta's management, and they made arrangements for her to perform at the evening candlelight service. On that April night the massive sanctuary was packed. Some of Washington's most powerful jammed the front pews eager to have their opposition to the war to be noted. The religious leaders inspired us with their remarks, and McCarthy amazed us with his quiet voice filling the church with his poetry. Then Odetta stood up and, gently strumming her own guitar, smiled and simply said, "We are in this together, aren't we?" Her strong, powerful, deep and even masculine voice boomed out against injustice, war and hate. With her first notes, both powerful and common people were caught in her spiritual web. In closing she sang "Let Us Break Bread Together." The audience stood and senators held hands with organizers, swaying and singing to her music.

Afterwards, I went up to her express my gratitude and her manager said, "This is the young man who insisted you sing this evening." To my amazement, she said, " Oh, I met him before, when he was organizing garbage workers. " Unable to control myself I said, "You couldn't remember that!" She smiled, hugged me again and pulled back with one of her hands on each of my shoulders. Looking me in the eye, she said, " I told you. You organize them and I will sing. Here we are again, David." One more hug and she added, " I'm tired and must go, but thank you for allowing me to serve."

With that she left my life, but her music has always played in my home and in my heart.

The Holiday Season

The cold has taken hold on Turkey Hollow, leaving no doubt that winter has arrived just in time for the holiday season. The wind chill has hovered at about five degrees for several nights, and that unmistakable cold northwest winter wind howls through the trees in the woods.

Only one week remains in the hunting season and so far so good for my clan. I'm keeping my fingers crossed that all of my favorite deer make it through the season.

The holiday spirit has arrived as well. I put lights out on the pine trees, and they look a little uneven, much to the dismay of my designer friends. Given the fact that maybe a grand total of forty people might see them throughout the entire holiday season, I thought, hell, they look good enough.

In the house, the tree is up early since I have to have surgery

just before Christmas. I wanted to enjoy it as much as I can. The fireplace is roaring and carols are filling the house. Steven baked some pies and the house smells like a gourmet bakery on the best street in Paris. My favorite decoration is the musical stuffed Santas and Snowmen that play carols when you push their plush stomachs. Everyone else hates them, even my cats. Steven keeps threatening to burn them if I push their stomachs one more time to hear "Silver Bells."

There are dozens of ornaments on the tree and each has its own history. Every year for several decades, my sister Patsy has given me a new Baccarat ornament. You should see them shimmering on the tree. There is a crucifix made out of pop beads that my mother made just before she passed away about twenty years ago. My dear friend Peter, who died of AIDS in 1989, gave me a set of toy soldiers so that I would always have men in uniform on the tree. Then there are the homemade decorations that my ex-boyfriend Patrick and I made on a houseboat in Amsterdam when we were cold and poor that year. I sit next to the fire and stare at the tree, filled with warm memories.

Winter comes with the holidays and we are preparing for a snow/ice event this weekend. That means we have to check the generator, get the salt ready, bring the shovels close to the porch and double check the snow blower. Brutal cold and howling storms never seem to respect holidays or travel schedules. We want the ambience of the snow but it always seems to come as you have to fly somewhere or while we wait for a visitor in the Hollow.

Peace

In many ways, "peace" has almost become a cliché.

Think about it. Peace is usually the first word out of any beauty pageant contestant's mouth. Hallmark Cards has made an entire industry off holiday cards with the word "peace" printed over beautiful white doves. Old hippies flash the peace sign and in a smokey haze mutter, "Peace, dude." Church choirs sing on Christmas Eve of "heavenly peace" and religious leaders are constantly looking for a new angle to give freshness to the greater concept of peace. New Age spiritual leaders give lectures on inner-peace. Many columnists have written about the peace of an empty home, absent the usual noise of their children. There are entire television channels consisting of nothing but a burning log or the ocean waves repeating themselves endlessly to create a so-called "peaceful ambience."

The holiday season is the time everyone embraces peace. One can be for peace and wish for an early return from Iraq for our soldiers and not get beaten up by some construction worker with a flag on their hat. I always love saying it every chance I get, but I still look over my shoulder to see if someone is going to let me have it. They think a proclamation of peace might be some left over Communist ideology from the old days. Stomp it out before it spreads too far and wide.

Today I found myself thinking about peace. My buddy Steven is in Hawaii with his family and I have the house to myself. The landscape is covered with snow and the deer are posing perfectly. There is a strange calm in these hills, and not a single tree is blowing in the wind. The road coming down from Old Man Keller's is very slippery today, so it is a good day to stay inside. In fact, I have to admit that I am still in my pajamas, being somewhat lazy today. Guess that is peace, too.

Peace is not a cliché for me. It is a way of life. My mother always said you have to live your life the way you want to see the world. Otherwise, how would you be able to describe it to others if you have never experienced it or seen it? So, I have attempted to the best of my ability to live a life of peace. In all aspects of my life from the way I treat my friends to my politics to caring for my neighbors. It is not always easy, but I do my best.

So this year, for the holidays, I will join the worldwide chorus and hope that our soldiers are all home to see the flowers in the spring. That the bloodbath in the Congo is ended and that children will play there instead of carrying US-built weapons. My vision includes an end to HIV/AIDS and other epidemics that have plagued our planet. Wouldn't it be more peaceful if we just accepted responsibility for our own spirituality and not demand everyone else believe it, too?

The music that is playing everywhere will give me joy and make me sing along (badly). The cards from Hallmark will make me smile, and I will put them out for others to see. My peace ornament is already on the tree. I will listen carefully at midnight Mass to hear what angle the pastor has come up with this year. The construction worker, the hippie, and I all will exchange a "Peace, bro," and I will do my best to tune the candidates out over the holidays.

Winter Returns and
Memories of Old Storms

After one the warmest Decembers in history, winter has returned in full force. This morning, the wind chill in Turkey Hollow was minus seven degrees, and the blowing snow looked like white sheets on a clothesline. While pouring my coffee, my eyes caught sight of nearly a dozen deer grazing in the brutal conditions in my backyard. At times they were barely visible through the blowing snow. Attila and Kate, given the extreme cold, had invited the neighborhood deer onto their turf. God must have given them some really special hides to live outside this time of year. They did seem to huddle together to block the thirty miles-per-hour winds, and I swear they seemed to give a collective group shiver.

Winter has also brought the Bald Eagles back, and people in town say that at least 150 are making themselves at home in the area. I'm still not used to looking in my backyard and seeing a majestic Bald Eagle posing for its close up.

This new phase of weather was ushered in last week by an ice storm. We got the tail end of it, and thankfully we didn't lose power. At times it looked like a Disney ice show with the trees totally coated in glistening ice. The set designers for the movie *Dr. Zhivago* couldn't have done any better. The only interruption of this beauty was the crackling sound of limbs getting ready to break as the trees swayed. Fortunately, their determination to stay strong in the face of howling winds kept them in one piece and my yard clear.

As my fireplace warmed my living room yesterday afternoon, I watched the magnificent show outside my window. I put down my book and drifted back to my childhood when every storm was a great adventure. As one gets older, memories tend to be a place of warmth, safety and amazement that we actually lived through certain experiences. Sometimes, remembering the hardships of youth can enable us to briefly forget the aches and pains of an aging body.

The great ice storm of 1958 was just such a time.

In 1958, the winter was tough, but by the end of March it was time for spring. On the farm, there was talk about how soon we could plant the pea crop. We were convinced that winter was over and chose to ignore Grandpa's warning that more winter was on the way.

The night of March 23rd reminded us to heed the wisdom of our elders.

Rain starting to fall and it was damn cold. Dad walked in from the machine shop where he was fixing tractors to get ready for the spring planting season. He had a look of concern on his face and said simply, "Mary, everything is freezing." We went to bed with heavy, rough Army blankets wrapped around us to keep warm. At that time, windows were insulated by stuffing cloth where the wind howled through. I used to love the sound of the wind blowing through the large pine trees outside my bedroom window. Never did that sound fail to put me to sleep.

I woke up on March 24th with Christmas-like anticipation. Looking out my window, I could see absolutely nothing. The window was so thickly coated with ice that it distorted the sunlight coming into my room like a prism. Dad, hearing me stir, shouted out, "Don't try to get the ice off the window. It will crack the pane." Mom was baking cinnamon toast and making some hot chocolate just as the power went out. Darkness filled the house. Dad went out to check on the farming division where we lived, and when he came back he said, "Every line is down and even the telephone poles are falling over. We are going to be without power for a long time." Soon, we heard branches breaking off trees.

At first, it seemed like a great adventure as we took out kerosene lamps and flashlights for the evening. The ice continued to thicken as more freezing rain fell. Throughout the day, the house got colder and colder, and I stayed in bed to get warm. Finally, the rain stopped but so did the fun. We wanted to be warm. Everything outside was covered with about an inch of ice… nothing was spared.

It wasn't until the next day that the full extent of the storm became clear, as we had no phone or radio. Mom and Dad decided to bring us to Grandpa Grove's house. Dad, slipping and falling, walked my older brother, Melvin, and me to the machine shop, where we found our old GMC pickup and packed the back of it with bags of seed to weigh it down. He stuffed us into the front seats (there were no seatbelts back then) and drove the truck across the lawn right up to our back door so Mom could jam herself in.

Aunt Evelyn and her five children were already living at Grandpa's house. The small two-story home was heated by a wood stove, on which they cooked their meals. The house was about two miles away, at a crossroads called Shirley, which consisted of their very fragile home, a country store, and another farmhouse.

Driving on the main roads was out of the question since wires and telephone poles littered the streets everywhere. We headed out across the fields, which were covered with a sheet of ice. At times the truck totally spun around in a circle like a cheap amusement ride. Mom would scream, Melvin and I would laugh, and Dad would cuss.

The truck couldn't climb the last hill and we walked the rest of the way. Grandpa's house was a small place, and we weren't quite sure that it could withstand a windstorm. The bathroom was an outhouse in the back, which was no fun getting to though the ice. There was a big wood stove in the kitchen for cooking and my job was to go to the woodshed and keep the flames fed. The living room was tiny considering there were ten of us, and keeping wood in the square wood stove that grandly intruded into the living room was a pain in the ass for the young ones. Besides, there was no way to gage the heat and the stove made the house either unbearably hot or too cold. In the evening, when we all went to sleep on the floor or in the beds, it was too hot in the living room and there was no heat upstairs. After five days, the power came on and we headed home. I was ready. The sense of adventure had long worn off and

getting the wood was no longer a "fun project." Slipping on the ice on my way to the outhouse and shivering inside as I went was my least favorite thing. But we all felt that we had pitched in as a family and survived the storm together. It was an amazing feeling.

Today, in my toasty living room, I know that if the power goes out my big ass 16,000-kilowatt generator will automatically kick in and the lights will stay on. My eight horsepower snow blower—my new toy—will clear the walks easily. My microwave will still work.

But when I want to remember that ice storm in 1958, I make cinnamon toast. And as the smell fills the house, I remember a different time when we all made it together.

The Joy of Winter

The citizens of Turkey Hollow (along with most of the rest of the nation) have been in the grip of a bitter cold wave. As I sit here with hot chocolate in the early evening writing, it is already two degrees below zero. Now I am telling you that it is cold. If I open the door it is like walking into an icy brick wall. God knows what the wind chill is currently. However, I have to be honest, I love winter—especially this winter.

I'm not one of those folks at the country store complaining about the brutal, bleak, dark and cold days of winter. Nor one of those sissy snowbirds who escape to Florida and often get caught watching the fruit producers turning on their fans in an attempt to save their oranges on a cold night—they just don't have my respect. The ones with the calendars that count off the days to the first days of spring clearly don't have the stamina to live in Turkey

Hollow. Things weather-wise can be tough in these hills, but they are supposed to be tough.

Now don't get me wrong. I struggle in it all. Getting up the dirt hilly road out of Turkey Hollow is one constant adventure with neighbors digging out cars that fail to make the incline. Some days we all just know that no car is going to make that hill and everyone might as well just light a fire and read a book. The propane gas truck won't come down the hill unless we can get the road totally clear since he can't make it back up the hill if there's even a bit of icy snow. We learned that one the hard way when he got stuck in my yard. The Federal Express and UPS drivers don't even attempt to make the trek down and just leave the packages in a truck at the top of the hill. Forget the old saying about the mail "neither rain, snow, sleet etc." We have to go into town to get the mail since winter delivery is not possible here. Life can be rough.

But there is the good part. Life is a constant challenge, there's a sense of camaraderie among the residents, something always exciting happening to gossip about and a sense of humor about the life we have chosen to live here in these hills. If you ask Wayne Keller who, having lived up here for decades is the dean of these hills, how this winter compares with others, he simply says, "I will let you know in May." Without Old Man Keller many of us wouldn't have made it through the first year since he has a way of imparting wisdom to stupid newcomers. Now I find I can advise others and it feels good to have been trained by him.

Blissful Ignorance

Having had one of the roughest winters in quite awhile, some of my neighbors down at the country store indicate this is "what it use to be like when we had real snows." Not sure what it used to be like but right now I am measuring over three feet of snow all around my home and another batch of snow is predicted this week, and the big issue is that they are starting to run out of places to store the plowed white stuff.

These are the kind of issues I love to embrace. Going into the local stores, you can bond immediately, even with strangers, about a common plight and the challenges that might lie ahead. There is no dissension in Johnny's Barbershop, just reminiscing when it was worse. Some old-timers laugh and say this is nothing and others counter with stats to prove this is indeed a tough winter. The common agreement seems always to be that the photogenic weather people on television are pretty clueless prognosticators. That brings a smile to the entire populace, a chuckle about how that is true, and then without hesitation they share with you their own forecast. Love being part of this dialogue.

In many ways, this takes me back to the time in America when folks had a reasonable time period to live in blissful ignorance before having to come to terms with reality. When you had no television, most national issues didn't hit your home until the paper was delivered by mail. You couldn't go on the computer and watch news happen in real time. If a plane were to, say, land in the middle of the Hudson River, you wouldn't get the full story until maybe a day or two later. Then you'd read the first person accounts, without pictures of the plane, using your own vivid imagination of the horror for the folks inside. Of course, rarely were there survivors.

Countries could invade other countries, tsunamis could sweep entire nations and scandals could rock the halls of power, but we always had a break until the news reached us. We had time to absorb it; we had a moment to reflect and react. We couldn't even fax our concerns because the fax didn't exist. You could send a telegram, but that was very expensive for most people and, besides, Western Union was usually associated with bleak news. The two most common responses were to go to a town meeting or sit down, right a hand-written letter, put a stamp on it and take it to the post office. As busy as people were just meeting the day-to-day demands of living, you usually really had to feel strongly about something to go to all that effort.

Heroes were important to us back then. We actually had ticker tape parades for men and women of bravery and courage and not a winning sports team. In some ways that was because we weren't inside the capsule with Astronaut John Glenn, and we could only imagine what it must have been like for him. We weren't in the plane with Lindbergh. Our imaginations again played a role in creating a brave pioneer on a remarkable journey. Now we watch them eat, dance with the stars and dodge hovering paparazzi. I guess we are lucky we don't have to watch them going to the bathroom. That familiarity takes the mystery out of it and makes it seem everyday.

Without cell phones, faxes, computers, and television, we actually could choose what was important and remain blissfully ignorant of other issues. Feeling urgently about someone's failure to pay his or her nanny taxes just wasn't on the radar. There was the fur coat that President Eisenhower's chief-of-staff, Sherman Adams, received, and Nixon with his "Checkers the dog" speech, but such stories took weeks to unfold. Sometimes it's just nice to have a break from it all. To chose your issues and only to have to care about them instead of the constant chatter and noise around us.

New Kids In Town

We're half way through winter, though the brutal months of February and March still lie ahead. The deer have been holding up, but there is change in the air. The big bucks have shed their antlers for the winter and the young yearlings are starting to develop their personalities and claim their place in the herds. The cute little fawns are becoming young bucks and does and seeking their rightful place.

This is not easy for Attila.

First, he had to survive hunting season and then he shed his massive eight-point rack in a terrible blow to his masculinity. Now, instead of being the dominant force in our backyard, he is like most any other deer—buck or doe. You can only distinguish him by calling out his name; he'll jerk his head upwards to acknowledge the call. It can't be easy for him.

He was Kate's beau last year, but now she is too busy raising her young twins to give him much attention. Without the rack, he just doesn't seem to be her type anymore. The twins follow Kate around everywhere. One has adopted her serenity, though the other is very timid and is literally scared of her own shadow. Kate seems to never give Attila the time of day anymore.

To make the situation worse for the proud buck, there are new stars in town.

First and foremost, there is "Baby."

We named this yearling Baby because she is smaller in height and a little heavier than the other young ones. Her fur is thick, and she seems to always have a mischievous smile. Well, cute little Baby has become the new kid on the block. She is totally fearless, challenging the older deer and demanding to be noticed.

Once in awhile, even in this serene setting, the deer will rise on their hind legs and start kicking at each other like kangaroos. Recently, as one deer was grazing, Baby pushed forward and challenged the other deer for its food. The much older and taller deer stood on his back legs to kick at Baby. When Baby raised herself to meet the challenge from the older deer, the young one found herself standing at about half the other deer's height. When she realized that she was clearly the small one in the match, she forgot about kicking and without hesitation, head-butted the other deer square in the belly. It ran off immediately and Baby triumphantly enjoyed her meal.

Attila is going to have his hands full with this one in the coming months. But I bet that once his extraordinary new antlers emerge over the next months, Attila will quickly be back in charge. Baby better not push her luck since I imagine Attila has a long memory.

We All Just Need to be Neighbors

As I drove around Turkey Hollow the other day, I listened to my satellite radio. Various people called into the station and were debating whether the Republican or Democratic version of "family values" represented the real America. Republican callers were full of righteousness, damnation and judgment. The Democrats, on the other hand, chose their words more carefully, but attempted to show that they too believed in family values.

Driving in the snow and cold (the wind chill hit minus twenty-eight degrees last night), I waited for that one caller to say: "Who in the hell wants government involved in our families?"

Isn't family life hard enough without the government involved? I smiled as I thought of a government mediator sitting at my family's kitchen table, trying to work out an accepted code of conduct. Although I come from a loving and caring family, we've been through a lot over the years. And the idea that government could make my family march like little kids in Catholic school had me doubling with laughter. There is no doubt in my mind that any arbitrator at my family's table would quickly qualify for worker compensation.

In the midst of this foolish "family values" debate, I think we should remember the common sense to be simply good neighbors. You know, in the days when pioneers settled America, the only people you could count on were your neighbors. They would trek miles on horseback to lend a hand. Taking care of each other was an "American tradition" on the frontier. They cared for each other and built a nation in the process.

The other day, my good friend Will Trinkle made the journey to Turkey Hollow from New York City. As we drove to Scallions for lunch (literally a little log cabin in the middle of nowhere), we encountered a road filled with fire trucks putting out a large fire consuming a small home. As the road cleared and we drove past, we thanked the volunteer firemen from Livingston Manor and Roscoe as they put their hoses away. I realized that I would rely on those same men if I ever had a problem in Turkey Hollow.

On the way back from lunch and after some of Scallions' incredible homemade chili, we passed the same scene and this time, dozens of vehicles lined the road. They were neighbors. And instead of horses, the mode of transport around here tends to be super-sized pickup trucks. As they gathered in the front yard, we could see that they had brought clothes, food and were already cleaning up the fire damage. We saw the compassion on their faces. To them, being there to console their neighbors was simply the right thing to do.

The image took me back to my childhood. When my sister Patsy was sixteen, she dated a high school jock named Richie Urion. One night as they were coming home, a car ran a stop sign and broadsided their car about a mile from home. The elderly neighbor who lived on the corner immediately called my mom and dad. They found their daughter in a dark, wet ditch with her bloodied head in our neighbor's lap.

My dad found out that night that no ambulance served people in our rural area. Apparently, there just weren't enough of us. He lifted Patsy, who was seriously injured, into his arms and delicately maneuvered her into the back seat of our Ford. When my father got home from the hospital, he sat at the kitchen table and tears fell down his face. "They wouldn't come get my Patsy," he said. "No one was there to come and get her." He was livid.

As Patsy and Richie recovered, my dad called together the men who worked on Mr. Seabrook's farm. He was determined that our town would have an ambulance service. The men and women who worked on the farm organized and raised enough money to buy a twenty-year-old white Cadillac ambulance. They cleaned it, took first aid classes and gave that old caddy to the town.

As a side note, I think they could have used a little more training. Years later when I was eighteen, I got seriously ill while visiting Michigan. My father and his friend Woody drove the ambulance all the way from New Jersey to bring me home. On the way back, we ran out of gas on the Ohio Turnpike. My lungs burned because I couldn't stop laughing.

Nevertheless, at the risk of sounding sentimental, my point is that we have a duty to bring back the America where we all are our each other's neighbors.

After Hurricane Katrina and the federal government's meltdown, Americans rallied and literally bypassed the feds so those urgently in need could get help. On the news, we saw people from all over the country drive in caravans to the gulf coast. Kids sold lemonade and truck drivers donated their big rigs. Rescue teams and volunteer fire departments traveled on their own dime to help.

While our government fiddled as New Orleans drowned, the American people responded in a way that moved many of us to tears. No one asked if the fresh water being trucked to the gulf coast was for white or black people. They just brought the water with love. It was magnificent to behold.

. After 9/11 and Katrina, we know that our nation is capable of great love. That the frontier spirit of being a good neighbor and caring for each other still exists. We know that as a people, we are good at heart.

A Northeaster Blizzard Journal

A blizzard is Turkey Hollow's version of the Rose Parade, Macy's Thanksgiving Parade and Carnival all wrapped into one. It's a metrological event that generates anticipation, preparation, excitement and in some cases, just plain old fear. For over a week, we followed increasingly dire forecasts. Needless to say, it was an exciting week as the "Valentines Day Blizzard" approached. (I love how we name blizzards and hurricanes to make them more dramatic).

Given all the anticipation, I decided to keep a little journal during the week in order to record the story of a blizzard in the Catskill Mountains.

Tuesday, February 13/11:30 A.M. 14 degrees; cloudy

I woke up this morning and immediately flew to my computer to see what my favorite weather site, accuweather.com, said in their morning forecast. Around bedtime the night before, they predicted less snow, with a mixture of sleet and freezing rain. No such good news this morning.

Sipping coffee in my pajamas while deer grazed outside my office window, I read that Turkey Hollow was in for a hell of a blizzard with eighteen to twenty-four inches of snow, temperatures in the single digits and winds up to forty miles-per-hour. Now that is a storm that deserves a name.

As I continued to read, Old Man Keller called from up the street. The unofficial mayor of Turkey Hollow wanted to be sure that the new city slicker in the Hollow knew how to handle himself. It was a reassuring and friendly call, but it was to the point. Old Man Keller said austerely that if you go out into the storm for any reason, call a neighbor to let them know and again upon your return.

In addition, he said it was okay to feed the deer in the storm. These winter storms can be as tough on them as storms in the cold Colorado plains are on cattle. They'll huddle somewhere in the woods, though no one knows where for sure. They have to hide from the coyotes since they can out run the deer in the snow.

Finally, he said, fill the car's gas tank and load the back with survival gear in case you have to head out into the storm.

Once again, Old Man Keller proved how fortunate I am to have him as a friend. And once I hung up, my four other neighbors called wanting to know if I needed anything and making sure I had their phone numbers.

I headed to town and along the long winding road next to the Willowemoc River, my neighbors were preparing. Cars were parked at the end of the long of drives so they were close to the road. Folks were hitching huge snowplows on the front of their SUVs or pickup trucks.

Honestly, I had plain, old snow plow envy. Make a note to myself next year, I thought: I'm going to have a big, old plow on the front of my SUV.

Road crews were out, scraping the final bits of snow and ice left over from previous lake-effect snows. Peck's Country Store was packed since most knew that up here in the mountains, you can be stuck at home for three or four days. As I wheeled my cart through the market, I got tidbits of advice of what to get. One thoughtful older woman stopped me and said, "You don't have candles in your cart." I pointed out that I was a proud owner of a Guardian 16,000-killowatt generator. She took my hand and smiled, saying, "You boys and your toys. Pick up some candles to be safe." Did I really look like that much of a newcomer? Maybe it was the fondue sauce I was looking at.

I also picked up six bushels of apples to take care of my family (the deer) out back. I had a feeling that they were going to need all they help they could get.

In the afternoon, Old Man Keller walked down to teach me how to use my brand new snow blower. But there was bad news. Keller couldn't get it to work because the something or other didn't match the other something or other. Now, after paying serious money for my toy, I won't be able to use it. That, of course, will be good news to the young Carlson boy, an entrepreneurial shoveler who will become instantly richer later in the week due to the failure of technology.

Old Man Keller also showed me how to park my car in the garage so I could get out. What a great neighbor. But he warned that if the blizzard hits as hard as they expect, we could be snowbound for several days. The road into Turkey Hollow is made of dirt and runs between two peaks at the top of a mountain. And the drive to my house is about a half mile along the length of the hollow down a steep hill.

Tuesday, February 13/9:10 P.M. 19 degrees; snow

It's just started to snow and I find myself staring at the snowflakes through the window, seeking a message. Is this really the beginning of the storm or is this just a snow squall teasing me like a Calvin Klein model staring at me from a billboard? It seems to be picking up and I feel excited, like a kid the night before Christmas.

Wednesday, February 14/5:00 A.M. 11 degrees; freezing rain and heavy sleet

We had about five inches of snow last night but now it has turned to heavy freezing rain and sleet. My heart sank, until I turned on the weather forecast. They said that it will change back to snow and we'll get at least another twelve inches before this evening with blizzard conditions. Dare I believe them any more?

Five brave deer appeared in the backyard and literally danced when I threw them apples from my back deck. For a moment, I wondered what in the hell was I doing on my deck in my pajamas in the middle of a storm throwing apples. But their reaction made it worthwhile. My cats think I am nuts and begged me to come back to bed to keep them warm.

Wednesday, February 14/9:00 A.M. 13 degrees; snow and sleet

Damn, it's still sleet with some snow mixed it. I am so disappointed that we won't get a blizzard but six to twelve inches of this mixed crap.

Wednesday, February 14/12:00 P.M. 29 degrees; sleet and freezing rain

Hell, this is getting depressing. The sleet has turned to freezing rain and despite the beauty of everything being coated with ice, this is just not the damn mountain blizzard I wanted. Old Man Keller called and said he is going to wait to plow since the sleet is so heavy. A couple of deer came up to the house for their allotment of apples but they looked so miserable. I wanted to gather the deer up, bring them inside, wrap towels around them and sit them by the fire. The two cats quickly vetoed that idea.

Wednesday, February 14/2:30 P.M. 26 degrees; heavy blowing snow

Well, the blizzard finally arrived. For the last couple of hours, the snow has fallen at a rate of two inches an hour with blowing winds. The whole process seems like one of those old fashion covered-dish supper Jell-O molds with muck at the bottom topped by a vivid white cream cheese. This is what I wanted all along, but somehow knowing that slush and ice are just underneath is disturbing.

Wednesday, February 14/8:00 P.M. 15 degrees; blowing snow

Wow, we finally got it from the tail end of the storm. We have seveteen inches of snow and the winds are howling up to forty miles-per-hour. My outside spotlights make the blizzard almost artful with all sorts of patterns swirling in the wind. It is like blowing smoke into a wind tunnel and being able to see the amazing patterns and directions that the wind takes. I am in heaven, and I know that being entertained is a good thing because I am totally snow bound and most likely will be for a day or two. Young Jesse Carlson called and asked if I was okay and offered to bring up anything I needed on snow mobile. The concept of being neighbors is such a powerful force up here.

Thursday, February 15/5:00 A.M. 2 degrees (-19 wind chill); blowing snow

I woke up this morning to the same delightful show. The deer, looking worse for wear, were waiting for some apples. As I fed them, I felt like the Coast Guard on a relief mission. There will be plenty of time to write today since I clearly am not going anywhere. The drive and road are completely drifted shut. What a week of excitement, fun and adventure. I simply love it up here.

Thursday, February 15/11:00 A.M. 4 degrees; blowing Snow

Old Man Keller called and he said that he had been out to Turkey Hollow Road. He said the conditions were the worst that he has seen in his thirty years on the mountain. The road can't be plowed because there is a layer of two to three inches of solid ice under a foot of snow. The plows can't crack the thick ice and hold the road. Seems that I might be up here awhile and nature has won.

I Can See

This week saw most people "looking through the eyes of love," as the old song says—giving flowers and chocolates and Valentines. In that spirit, I gave myself some long over-due cataract surgery. While not especially romantic, it was eye opening. Literally.

Who knew that my house was painted a bright lemon-yellow? That my cat had spots? And wait until I find that furniture salesman who sold me an orange Naugahyde sofa instead of the sexy, brown leather Restoration Hardware sectional I pointed out in the catalogue.

But seriously, there's no way to describe my surprise and delight when I finally could see clearly again. Coming back to Turkey Hollow from the surgery, my face was plastered to the window of the car as I once again discovered the nuances of color, depth and detail. It was as though I was seeing things for the first time as the outside world unfolded to me in glorious crystal clear vision. Like HD-TV for the pupils. Because of my struggle with my throat tumor at the end of last year, I had postponed having my cataracts removed. By the time Dr. Coad got me in the operating room, my vision had gotten so bad that, for months, life for had been one, big, creamy blur.

The thought of someone operating on my eyes didn't exactly thrill me. Having Dr. Coad, who is viewed as one of the best in the business, helped to calm my nerves but I still wasn't wild about the idea. But I knew it was time for surgery when driving down Turkey Hollow I mistook a mailbox for a deer.

What I didn't know was how easy it is, with the right surgeon, to successfully remove cataracts. You go into the hospital, get into the gown with the drafty open back, have a few tests and then wait. Finally, onto a stretcher you go, wheeled down to a parking space outside the operating room for your turn. Before you know it—bingo!—you are inside. While chatting with medical team, you are painlessly operated upon and within a half an hour you're outside in the recovery room. If you would have—or could have— blinked, you would have missed it.

They give you a warmed-up muffin and coffee in the recovery room just like the old days when you gave blood at the local blood bank. A little leather kit with a regimen of eye drops and a really cool pair of sunglasses make up your post-op gift bag. I ended my day back in my dark hotel room watching *Enchanted*, the modern day *Cinderella*, and falling asleep wondering if my eyesight would be much better in the morning.

Well, I hate to employ the hoary gay cliché, but I woke up feeling like Dorothy going from the dull black and white of

Kansas to the dazzling Technicolor of Oz. It was extraordinary. Days later, I still can't stop looking at everyone and everything, taking it all in, comparing and contrasting, examining every fine detail. If I didn't know better, I would swear they had slipped me some mushrooms or psychedelic drug. The colors and textures were jumping out at me, and I could see road signs again. No more heading to D.C. when I thought I was going to New York.

Most of all, I am just totally grateful for science, good doctors and rejoining the world of beautiful colors.

Now, about moving out that orange sofa...

So Close Yet So Far Away...

"Close only counts in horseshoes" goes the old country saying. Given this winter's constant and endless brutality here in these hills, spring seems so close yet so far away. Starting about a week ago we ended up having another unpredicted storm with sixteen inches of snow over four days and howling winds. Over the Shandalee Pass, where they had to use front loaders to clear the drifts, the snow is twice as high as my car. The howling winds created drifts that came right up over my porch, which is six feet high off the ground.

Old Man Keller was on full-time duty clearing and keeping the road passable. When I had to get out to take my cat, Kansas to be fixed at the vet, I had our country road hills sanded to help with traction. That brought loud and amusing guffaws from Keller who called me "chicken" for not attempting to make it out

with my four-wheel drive. He was right. Still have just enough city in me not to want to attempt the famous Turkey Hollow Hill. Kansas' welfare gave me the excuse, but actually I was afraid of going into a drift and having to dig my way out. Of course he was right. He still knows these hills better than I ever will.

The bitter cold ensured that all three of my cats huddled together in bed creating warmth for each other. They look at the window and can only think of past times on the screened porch where they could lay in the sun, watch the deer graze in the sunflowers and get angry at the birds who would torment them on the other side of the screens. I have to say I am now on the cats' side. My love of snow is well known, and I am thrilled to see it coming down, especially in an old fashioned blizzard. But this is the year that has tested my patience with well over seven feet of snow having fallen in these hills.

Along with the cats, I now sit at the window and long not for beautiful snow but the absence of winter. I yearn to sit on my back porch, having a light supper, reading my favorite book, seeing the deer lie in the wildflowers, turning on the outdoor fireplace at night and rock in my chair listening the night sounds and watching the lightening bugs. I am ready—*real* ready—for spring.

All the more frustrating as it seems so close. The winter has been so brutal that we keep telling ourselves that we will have an early spring. So far, that has been only wishful thinking. Knowing under all that snow, that the daffodils might be peeping out makes you want to get on your hands and knees and dig down to them just to see that first spray of beautiful yellow. Sound desperate?

You bet.

Hanging On

You ever have those times in life you felt like you were just hanging on. That no matter what you do to embrace your life journey, nothing seems to move in the right direction for you? You even wonder at times if this is all there is to life and if you will ever get to the other side of your stagnation.

We all have had those times in our life and the issue is not avoiding them but how to deal with them.

During the past couples of weeks, I have watched the deer emerge from winter. Fortunately, the first half of the season was mild but the last three months have been brutal. Some deer barely made it through. When they showed up in my backyard after the heavy snows and bitter cold, many were skin and bones. I wondered what they called upon inside themselves to survive these last dark weeks to make it to spring. But this week, their flesh is fuller, they are playing and dancing in my backyard and they seem thrilled to bask in the spring sun.

Even the daffodils are an enigma. Every other blooming flower wilts in a frost or heavy snow. But the daffodils are determined to be the flower that announces spring—pushing upward no matter if they are covered in snow or if they have to endure one more bitterly cold night. This week, with new blooms, they once again achieved the honor of declaring that spring had arrived. These yellow flowers standing beneath my yellow house bring lightness to my mountain woods, creating my own Walden Pond. It makes my heart sing.

They all hang on to give us their gifts and somehow they know that it will get better. That nature has a certain order and it will be all right.

Mahatma Gandhi always knew when he needed to pull back and hang on until it was clear how he was supposed to continue his journey. Often when talks between Muslims and Hindus were difficult and stalled, he would get up from the negotiating table and simply return to his Ashram. There, he would make the traditional Indian *dhoti* and shawl woven with a *charkha*. He called this time his "wilderness years," and he had the wisdom not to return to activism until he was certain what he had to say and if people were ready to listen.

I personally have had those times in life where I felt if I was just hanging on and it was sheer blind faith that enabled me to walk through fear to get to the other side. My younger years were actually a dark time for me, filled with fear, low self-esteem and failure. Those demons seemed to rule my soul, but when the light finally returned to my life, I almost forgot they ever existed.

As I have grown older, I am still not particularly fond of my "wilderness years." Now I find that I am no longer afraid of them. Spring is just down the road and there is always a time and place for one of my gifts. Instead of depression and fear, I fill the time with the search for knowledge, listening to music, spending time with my teachers and reading the books of others who had to struggle through difficult times. I usually emerge into my own personal spring rejuvenated and filled with strength.

Hanging on can be a place of real opportunity. A place for personal growth and, like the deer, a place to find one's own courage to survive. It can be a time out to gain new knowledge and to deepen personal bonds between those you love and yourself.

I kept this line from Gandhi close to me during my own wilderness years:

"When I despair, I remember that all through history the way of truth and love has always won. There have been tyrants and murderers and for a time they seem invincible, but in the end, they always fall — think of it, always."

Regrets

"Non, je ne regrette rien"

As I am writing this morning and listening to the songs of the "Little Sparrow"—Edith Piaf—my mind starts drifting back over my life. Can't think of a better place to reflect on life's "regrets" than Turkey Hollow. With spring encroaching into the mountains and the snow melting, it is almost impossible to be depressed about any aspect of life's journey. The concept of "if I had to live life over I wouldn't make any changes" is just ridiculous to me. Yes, each and every experience has created this person I am today. There is no question but that my end result so far is pleasing to me; however I do have regrets.

What is important to realize is that with each regret has come great gifts. Simply by embracing those gifts has enabled me not to become a victim or dwell on the negative past.

Foremost among them, is wishing that the closet door would have swung open far quicker than it did. Missing so much of my wonderful sexuality in youth through low self-esteem, lies and self-hatred for being gay is something that has brought a good deal of sadness to me. Coming out sooner and having the courage to celebrate my total being would have led to such a magnificent journey. With this realization, I have absolutely refused in my later years to allow others to suppress my sexuality. Whatever was missed in my youth is being reflected in an extraordinary journey in my more senior years.

Having lost so many friends in the HIV/AIDS epidemic has formed my entire life. Never will I, no matter what people tell me, feel I did enough to save their lives. Feeling totally powerless watching one friend after another disappear into the light was a total horror. Waking up each morning, caring for one friend, burying another friend and heading to the Sherman Oaks AIDS ward to visit yet one more friend was my existence for over a quarter of my adult life. More than any other period, it has formed every second of life since then. Whether it is simply missing a huge number of dear loved ones or growing old without peers, AIDS is as much a part of who I am as is the sun.

Took me some time to find the gift in that dark period, but there was indeed a powerful one, because eventually I realized my choice was either to become a victim of the epidemic wearing black the rest of my life or embrace the gift of life that I have been given not only for myself but with the energy of all my departed friends. That realization, that gift has enabled me to take chances, constantly be grateful, celebrate life daily, laugh all the time and not fear death.

Right up there on my list of regrets is the Great Peace March in 1986. Excerpts from an interview with *Metro Weekly* honestly reflect my feelings on this massive disappointment.

MW: In 1986, you conceived of the Great Peace March for Global Nuclear Disarmament, in which thousands marched across the country from Los Angeles to Washington, D.C. It was one of your biggest non-gay ventures.

MIXNER: Yeah. And the biggest political failure of my life. It was, in some ways, a success, but not because of me.

MW: Why?

MIXNER: Ego. Pure and simple. You start believing what people tell you at a young age. So instead of defining yourself and your own journey and the path that God has chosen for you, I started living the expectations of how people said they saw me. And my ego got out of control.

Fortunately, I had directed my ego to a good cause—nuclear disarmament. The concept of the March was good and the cause was good. But the decision-making apparatus within the organization was flawed because of my ego. And it failed in the way I had planned it. Now the wonderful, magnificent part about this story is that the marchers reorganized on their own and continued to walk across country, despite the burden I had placed on them.

It is without a doubt my biggest political failure and one of my biggest regrets. Years later, I still get shaky every time I talk about it. But I have some pride in how I handled it. I didn't blame others. I didn't hold fundraisers afterwards to ask people to raise money—I paid off four hundred and some thousand dollars worth of small debt on my own over the next five years.

Outside the HIV/AIDS crisis, the greatest gifts in my life came from the results of this march. There were so many powerful lessons. How painful they came to me have become increasingly irrelevant over the years. Am I free of ego now? Hell, no. However, I am able to step back and put my ego in its proper place 99% of the time. My understanding of what "community" is all about has my total respect now. Being humbled and humiliated for my ego-driven actions certainly has served as a healthy check as my journey proceeded after that event.

I realize that while I have regrets they are far overshadowed by the lessons, the wisdom gained and the resulting joy. While only a partial list of my regrets, I guess I can listen to Edith and sing *"Non, je ne regrette rien"* and feel it and believe it.

Afterward

꙰

Over a year has passed since health considerations required me to move from my beloved home in the wilderness back to the city. Visits with doctors had become so frequent that it was no longer convenient nor advisable to live hours away, not to mention I couldn't risk what might happen in the event of an emergency. The nearest hospital was twenty-two miles on winding roads, so imagine the time it would take to dispatch an ambulance and have it return. I had no choice but to return to New York City.

With the arrival of the new spring blossoms, I'm reminded how much I miss my bucolic Catskills hideaway. How could anyplace ever again compete with the natural wonders of my old home? Once familiar fields of wildflowers were suddenly nowhere to be found, and the only animals I now encountered were ones walked on leashes or pulling carriages in Central Park. Forget about the smell of the woods, especially after a good rain. Here it was the smell of cabs and foods cooked on street corners. Gone was the quiet of the night, the creature sounds of coyotes and owls heard in the distance. Even the night sky looked different from my the apartment in Times Square, where the light pollution from all billboards and hotels drown out the possibility of viewing the millions of stars hidden behind the haze of light. To be sure, New York is exciting as ever and I was glad to be back, connecting with friends. Still, I missed country life and all my animal friends who populated it. Who would throw Attila and Kate apples now that I had left? I tried not to think about it.

But the city can be a funny place, full of life but at the same time lonesomeness, too. In the Hollow, I actually felt less alone than I do in Manhattan. I could count on visitors everyday, even in the brutal winter months. Of course, most of them were animals, but they were my friends and always happy to see me. Apart from that I had the people of Turkey Hollow looking after me. My friends in the Hollow tended to be available when you needed them. But I didn't need to see people every day. Just knowing that Old Man Keller was down the hill anytime I needed him made a difference. There was also a reverence for the elderly that seems to be missing in the city.

I've jumped right in to this new chapter of my life. Manhattan has so many marvelous adventures to offer and—sometimes with a little hesitation because I don't know if the body can always keep up with the demands—I'm doing my best to take advantage of as much as possible. My retreat from the world has allowed me to return to the city with fresh eyes and a new appetite for discovery. My time is filled with creative people and those making change. I love having my intellect stimulated every day. Having a marvelous conversations with friends around a table, dissecting life until the late hours, is a delightful treat. I'm a little older and a little wiser because of my time in the country. Turkey Hollow taught me to continue to celebrate the wonders of life whether in nature or in busy city streets. Life is a gift and never should be squandered. Although I still miss all the many friends who are no longer with us, their memories live with me. Life goes on, and so do I.

Acknowledgments

As always with these publishing endeavors there are people who I have to extend deep thanks for making the publication of *At Home with Myself* possible.

First and foremost is Don Weise, who is a gift from God. Every author should be so fortunate to encounter someone in publishing who is not only a talented publisher and editor but a kind, thoughtful and wise man. I just adore him.

Second, my deep thanks to Judith Light for the extraordinary and generous Preface. I am so honored and grateful.

Finally, to Alan Cumming and Urvashi Vaid for reading the book and providing comments. You are such good friends.

And thank you to my family, friends, doctors and cats for being there for me all the time.